POSITIVE & ENCOURAGING moments for MOMS

POSITIVE & ENCOURAGING *moments for* MOMS

GRACE *from* GOD'S WORD *for* EVERY SEASON *of* MOTHERHOOD

Written by

SUZANNE GOSSELIN

K-LOVE BOOKS

Positive and Encouraging Moments for Moms:
Grace from God's Word for Every Season of Motherhood

Written by Suzanne Gosselin

Published by K-LOVE Books, a partner of Forefront Books, Nashville, Tennessee.
Distributed by Simon & Schuster.

Library of Congress Control Number: 2025927529

Print ISBN: 978-1-63763-536-0
E-book ISBN: 978-1-63763-537-7

Cover Design by Greg Jackson/Thinkpen Design
Interior Design by Mary Susan Oleson, Blu Design Concepts

Printed in the United States of America
26 27 28 29 30 31 VEP 10 9 8 7 6 5 4 3 2 1

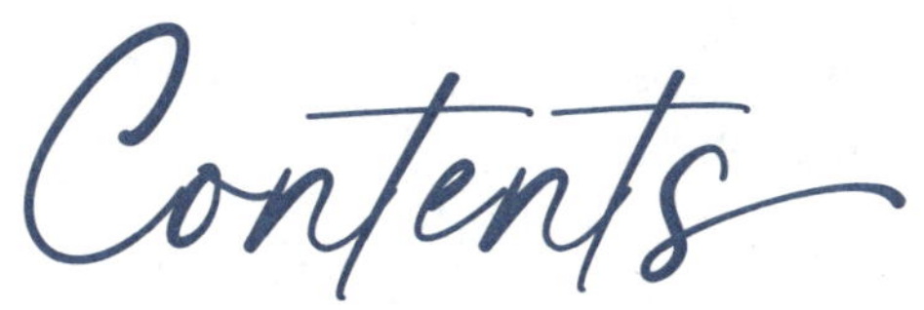

Foreword

BY CECE WINANS

Motherhood is the most terrifying, magnificent, overwhelming, rewarding role I've ever filled. From the moment my son, Alvin III, was placed in my arms, I felt the full weight of my inadequacy to raise this little human. I instantly recognized that I needed God's divine help to rise above my shortcomings as a mom and guide my son. Then came Ashley, a completely different little human, with a different personality and needs. And she tested me more than her brother (bless her)! I needed an extra dose of wisdom to guide her down the unique path God had for her.

When I was the young mom of two toddlers, there were many days when I felt depleted. So many people needed things from me, and I was stretched so thin.

During that season, I often felt like my own wants and needs were selfish. When that check engine light of my soul would come on because I was exhausted, irritable, or dropping the ball, I'd ignore it and keep driving. Then I'd feel like I was letting everyone down, and mom guilt would ensue. I needed the truth of God's Word to steady me and remind me of my mission: to lovingly raise my kids in the knowledge of the Lord. I also needed the wisdom, prayer, and tangible encouragement that came from my mom and the older women in my life. How grateful I am for their investment in me as I learned to navigate the sacred role of motherhood with all its ups and downs.

I was fortunate to learn from the best. My sweet mom, Delores Winans, would work all day as a medical transcriptionist at the hospital and then come home to train and nurture her brood. I remember her presence and availability. She would have conversations with us, sew our outfits, and help us prepare for school the next day. In the morning, she would pray with us, commissioning us to live for Christ in whatever challenges we would face that day at school.

When I was growing up, I wanted to be exactly like my mother. Even as a child, I understood that her beauty came from God dwelling in her. The law of kindness was on her tongue. I never had to guess what it meant to be a godly woman or question my mom's deep love for Jesus. Her example made me want to be a present and prayerful mom. When my kids were growing up and I had a regular tour schedule, I made it a priority to fly home after many concerts so that I could spend time with my family. I wanted to be there in the morning to have breakfast with my kids and pray for them before they went to school.

A mother's role matters greatly. In fact, research reveals that moms are the biggest influence on their children's spiritual journey and decision to follow Jesus. God has given mothers a defining role in their children's lives and spiritual development. And you must expect that the enemy will seek to trip you up in this important, sacrificial work. When my kids were growing up, there were some hard days (especially when they were teenagers). When I felt overwhelmed or stressed, I would call my mom or the older ladies at my church, and they would encourage me, pray for me, point me to God's Word, and remind me that I was not alone.

That's exactly what this devotional is meant to do. It contains the voices of mothers at all stages of the journey—some with young children, others with teens, and some whose kids are grown. None of us are perfect or have motherhood figured out, but all of us desire to see mothers thrive. I'm thankful for my own precious mother, and now my daughter, Ashley, is a mother, which makes me a grandma. It's amazing how much time, energy, and attention those sweet little babies require. Wherever you are on the journey, God goes with you. The moms in these pages are cheering you on, too!

A Message to Readers

HAVE YOU EVER had one of those days? You pull into your child's doctor's appointment ten minutes late. You drag a screaming toddler out of the grocery store. You forget to pick up your teen from soccer practice. You open the fridge at breakfast to discover an empty milk carton.

Motherhood is hard! At some point or another, most of us have asked ourselves questions like, *Am I doing this right?* or *Is every other mom doing this better than me?* It only takes a minute or two on social media to compare ourselves to the supermoms around us and start wondering if we measure up.

Motherhood is demanding, beautiful, unpredictable, and downright tiring. Baby cuddles on lazy mornings. Witnessing the absolute wonder of a child's curious, developing mind. Teaching a teenager to drive. Dropping a young adult off at college. Watching a daughter walk down the aisle. The assignment seems to be constantly changing as we scramble to keep up with growing bodies, expanding minds, and mounting emotions.

And the journey of being a mother never ends. It's a lifelong calling. Psalm 127 describes children as arrows that mothers and fathers launch into the world to accomplish great things. That's a *big* deal. We are raising the next generation who will show the world Jesus's love.

The thoughts and testimonies in this book are intended to inspire you to be the mom God designed you to be. You don't have to be like any other mom. In His wisdom, God knew the children you would have long before they were born, and He has specially equipped you to be their mom. Whether you're a mom of littles, older children, or those already out of the house, the nuggets of truth, Scripture, and quotes from some of your favorite K-LOVE artists contained in this book are meant to fortify you in the daily grind and remind you of your identity in Christ. We're in this together, and you, Mom, have been fully equipped for the task.

*In His wisdom,
God knew the
children you would
have long before
they were born,
and He has
specially equipped
you to be their mom.*

Top Recruit

The one who calls you is faithful,
and he will do it.

1 Thessalonians 5:24

Have you ever felt like there's too much day left at the end of your strength? The baby won't take his afternoon nap. Dad is coming home late from work. The house looks like a demolition site. The girls need to be picked up from dance class. And the washing machine is broken.

Maybe in the craziness of mom life, you've thought, *This is not what I signed up for!*

If you've been there, you're not alone. Being a mom is arguably one of the most demanding seasons in a woman's life. Maybe you imagined motherhood looking different (and simpler) than it is. Perhaps you imagined *yourself* looking different as a mom than you do. You may find yourself wondering if you would have signed up for this had you known all that was required.

In many areas of life, we enlist—we accept job offers, volunteer for organizations, or enroll in classes. But we don't sign up for motherhood. Yes, we may choose to bring a child into the world, or make one part of our family through adoption, but we are *recruited* by God to be that child's mother. How incredible to think that you are specifically chosen to be *your child's* mother.

At times motherhood can seem like a mammoth calling, but God equips us for the task. Ephesians 2:10 tells us: "For we are God's handiwork, created in Christ Jesus to do good works, which God prepared in advance for us to do." Being a mom to your child is one of the good works God has prepared for you to do.

Whether you're just beginning your day or finishing up a stressful one, remember that God has recruited you. And He'll help you do all the wonderful things He has planned.

"There are few assignments in human experience that require the array of skills and wisdom needed by a mom in fulfilling her everyday duties."[1]

—Dr. James Dobson

Remember This

God has called you to be your child's mother. He will be faithful to help you accomplish all He has planned and provide for your every need. Trust in His wisdom and knowledge today.

Leaning Into the Spirit

In the same way, the Spirit helps us in our weakness. We do not know what we ought to pray for, but the Spirit himself intercedes for us through wordless groans. And he who searches our hearts knows the mind of the Spirit, because the Spirit intercedes for God's people in accordance with the will of God.

Romans 8:26–27

There are times as a mom when we simply do not know what to do for our children. We don't always know what our children need or how to help them. We may not even know how to pray for them.

When CeCe Winans was raising her children, Alvin Love III and Ashley Rose, she regularly depended on the Holy Spirit in parenting dilemmas.

"When my young adult son moved to Australia to get space from us and do his own thing, my husband and I had to let him go and trust his path to the Lord," she writes in her book *Believe for It.* "But as I prayed for God's will to be done in my son's life, the Holy Spirit, knowing all the hearts involved, and the mind of God—joined me in my pleas. What an extraordinary gift God offers us through His Holy Spirit!"[2]

As mothers, we have a powerful helper in the Holy Spirit. No two children are the same—they have different personalities, needs, and motivators. As we ask the Holy Spirit for wisdom and discernment to parent our children, He will be faithful to lead and guide us. He may prompt us to ask a question, offer compassion, or investigate a situation more thoroughly. The insights He provides can lead to major breakthroughs.

We can't save our children or fix all their problems, but we can point them to the *One who can.* When our children face heartache, peer pressure, or challenges, God's Spirit gives us discernment on how to guide them with gentleness, grace, and truth. In challenging conversations, He will give us the words to speak and the courage to act decisively. On the journey of motherhood, God's Holy Spirit is there day and night offering help and hope.

"When I think back on some of the more difficult discussions I've had with my children, I can see how when my heart was right, the Spirit gave me exactly the right words to say. In fact, sometimes I'm surprised at what He said through me. Thanks to the Holy Spirit, we don't have to be great theologians or orators to effectively guide our children through the truths of God's Word."[3]

—CeCe Winans

Remember This

The Holy Spirit is one of our greatest parenting resources. He provides wisdom, power, and strength. He supports us in our weakness and intercedes on our behalf to help us raise our children according to God's will.

Childlike Faith

I tell you the truth, anyone who doesn't receive the Kingdom of God like a child will never enter it.

Luke 18:17 (NLT)

Children have a knack for trusting God. Whether they're praying for the sun to come out so they can play outside or seeking God on behalf of a sick neighbor, they pray with deep conviction, believing God will answer their requests—and He does! Jesus said that the angels of children always see the Father's face in heaven (Matt. 18:10). God loves children and honors their faith.

One day while Jesus was teaching, He used a young child as an object lesson to demonstrate the kind of faith required to enter His kingdom. The gospel is so simple that even a child can understand it, but receiving salvation requires humility and trust—qualities that children have in abundance.

Some days we may find ourselves preoccupied with teaching and training our little ones, but when we pay attention, they can teach us about faith. They believe that God cares about the little things—like owies, sick grandmas, and lost pets. As adults we may censor our prayers, saving only the "worthy" requests for God, but children tell Him everything! He cares about everything and loves to hear His children's requests.

First Peter 5:7 says, "Give all your worries and cares to God, for he cares about you" (NLT). He invites us to bring our worries to Him with childlike faith—trusting that He will act. Just as we care for our children, He cares for us. No worry is too small to bring to Him in simple, childlike faith.

"Motherhood is the daily practice of entering the world of a child. To have to remember what it's like to be a child. . . . It's such a life hack for childlike faith."

—Rachael Lampa

Remember This

Mothering can teach us about approaching God like children—with humility and trust.

Long Days, Short Years

Teach us to number our days,
that we may gain a heart of wisdom.

Psalm 90:12

As a mom, it's easy to get lost in the daily grind—endless laundry, perpetual school pickups, and bedtime routines that seem to last forever. The days can feel long, repetitive, and sometimes overwhelming. Yet within these mundane moments, God has given us a precious gift: time.

It's mind-boggling to think that we get approximately 936 weeks from the time our child is born to the time he leaves home (that means if you have a kindergartner, you have around 667 weeks remaining!).[4] That might seem like a lot—until you realize how quickly those weeks go by.

The baby with the gummy smile grows into the kindergartner with a backpack and, before you know it, a teen with a learner's permit. The sleepless chaos of the baby and toddler years gives way to full nights of sleep—and big kids who eat you out of house and home.

Experienced mothers will tell you, "The days are long, but the years are short." It's true. The hard, messy, beautiful years of motherhood *don't* last forever. But this reality doesn't have to leave us feeling sad; it can fill us with purpose.

When we learn to number our days, as the psalmist encourages, we gain wisdom and begin to cherish our present experience—even the challenging parts. We might read one more book at bedtime, pause to listen to our child ramble on about his day, leave the pile of dishes in the sink in favor of a walk or a board game, or snuggle just a little longer.

A friend once posted a picture of herself and her young children at a park. "These are the good old days," she wrote. For many of us, that may turn out to be true—not because every day was perfect but because each one was overflowing with love.

So take a breath and ask God to help you see time the way He does—finite and infinitely precious. Make the most of each day. You have been chosen for this moment, so be present and savor it.

"Be happy in the moment, that's enough. Each moment is all we need, not more."

—Mother Teresa

Remember This

God gives us wise perspective when we recognize that time is limited. Seeing time the way He does inspires us to embrace the present and seize every opportunity to love the people in our lives.

The Ministry of Presence

Be devoted to one another in love.
Honor one another above yourselves.

Romans 12:10

Madison Cain Johnson, a mom of two boys and a member of the Christian Contemporary Music (CCM) trio CAIN, can't believe she gets to make music and tour with her adult siblings. While life on the road can get hectic, Madison considers her work a dream job.

"I'm grateful for the bond I share with my siblings," she says. "They are my best friends. And I get to watch them love my kids like their own."

Growing up as pastor's kids in Alabama, the Cain siblings picked up a lot from their parents, including faith, music, and a passion for family connection. From vacations, to living room jam sessions, to family dinners and late-night conversations, Madison recalls the security she felt, knowing her parents were always there for her.

Motherhood is a ministry of presence. Being a mom is more than just running schedules and checking off tasks from a list; it's being engaged and available. This may mean putting down the phone or setting work aside for an impromptu adventure or unplanned conversation.

As moms, we supply our children with a sense of security, comfort, and belonging. We not only provide for their physical needs, but we also nurture their emotional and spiritual development in ways that model God's love for us.

Isaiah 66:13 says, "As a mother comforts her child, so will I comfort you."

When we show our children that we're there for them—and don't make them work for our attention—we help them better understand God's comforting presence and unconditional love.

Madison, who is a hands-on mom and loves spending time with her two sons, is grateful for the example her parents set of being there for their kids. Her mom's ministry of presence continues to be a blessing in her life.

"Growing up, I felt that our parents preferred us. Many nights I would be up late talking to Mom and Dad. I'm sure they were tired and just wanted me to go to bed, but I never got that feeling from them. I want my boys to feel the same way—that I never grow tired of spending time with them."

—Madison Cain Johnson

Remember This

Motherhood is a ministry of presence. As you engage with your children through shared experiences and intentional conversation, you model God's devotion and unwavering presence.

6

In Search of Soul Care

He heals the brokenhearted
and binds up their wounds.
Psalm 147:3

Have you ever had *that* kind of week? The kind of week where everything feels heavy? The kids are irritable, the schedule is overstuffed, the car breaks down, and the demands keep coming like waves crashing on the shore. You feel exhausted, emotionally worn thin, and desperately in need of God's peace.

As moms, we carry so much physically, emotionally, and spiritually. And sometimes in the middle of the chaos, we feel the enemy trying to sneak in. Whether it's in parenting frustrations, relationship tensions, or rogue lies about our worth, it can feel like we're losing ground in our faith. But the opposite is true: In that place, God can do such amazing things.

He isn't waiting for you to pull it together. When you come to Him in rough shape—overwhelmed, in need of sleep, and feeling defeated—He meets you there. He's more than a quick fix. He offers long-term healing and rest as the soul-care specialist you so desperately need.

Maybe you've walked through a wooded path and marveled at God's greatness. Or perhaps you've stood by the ocean, breathed in the cool salty air, and remembered His grandeur. There's something about the majesty of nature that resets the soul. It reminds us that God's power is bigger than our problems. He faithfully holds us together through the storms of life.

"The Creator, Savior, Almighty, Sovereign King is with you. Let your heart rest. You are not in this parenting drama alone."[5]

—Paul David Tripp

Remember This

If you're having "one of those weeks" be reminded that God is near. He knows every care. He understands every worry. Let Him tend to your heart and soul with His great power.

Whether you're just beginning your day or finishing up a stressful one, remember that God has recruited you. And He'll help you do all the wonderful things He has planned.

7

Nurturing Adventure

The thief comes only to steal and kill and destroy; I have come that they may have life, and have it to the full.

John 10:10

Everything feels magical to a child—a new grocery store becomes a grand adventure, and bubbles drifting through the air inspire awe. As moms, we're blessed with a front-row seat to our children's wonder. Watching them splash in the ocean for the first time or examine a bug with wide-eyed curiosity reminds us that God created us for a life full of discovery and joy.

Taylor Cain Metz, a mom of two boys and one of the other sibling members of the CCM trio CAIN, says that one of the things she loves most about touring with her family is the new places they get to explore together.

"I feel like we've seen the coolest playgrounds and children's museums across the whole country!" Taylor says.

She has fond memories of adventuring with her parents and siblings as a kid and loves rediscovering the world through the eyes of her own kids. In John 10:10, Jesus said that He came so we might have life—and have it to the full. Following Jesus is never boring. Our Savior invites us into an adventurous journey with Him—an important truth we can pass on to our kids.

Don't allow the busyness of life to dim your sense of wonder. God calls you to live fully in both the extraordinary and mundane moments of your day. If you're stuck in a rut, try packing a picnic lunch, hiking a nearby trail, or exploring a new park. These outings create opportunities for fun, connection, and joy.

As you explore new places with your children, you're not only making memories—you're giving them a glimpse of the vibrant, abundant life Jesus offers and allowing God to refresh your own heart in the process.

"I have many wonderful memories of going on adventures with my family. That time together was huge. I always felt like Mom and Dad wanted us around. It helped me walk in confidence knowing I was wanted and loved."

—Taylor Cain Metz

Remember This

God invites us to a life of adventure and purpose. When we explore with our children and nurture their sense of wonder, we give them a glimpse of the exciting, abundant life Jesus offers.

Strength for Hard Days

But he said to me, 'My grace is sufficient for you, for my power is made perfect in weakness.' Therefore I will boast all the more gladly about my weaknesses, so that Christ's power may rest on me.

2 Corinthians 12:9

Motherhood is a beautiful and challenging journey, full of victories and defeats—for many of us, often within the same day! Some days we feel like we've got it all together, and other days we wonder how we're even keeping it together. And yet, every day we're called to love and nurture the children God has given us.

We all have areas of motherhood where we excel, as well as tasks that stretch us far beyond our comfort zones. Maybe it's meal planning, school drop-offs, keeping the house tidy, or having tough conversations. Whatever the challenge, as moms many of us feel the pressure to "do it all." When we feel like we're failing, it's easy to doubt our abilities and even question our worth. We can start to think that if we're not "killing it" as moms, then we're somehow failing.

Here's the beautiful reality: God works through our weaknesses. In fact, it's often in our weakest moments that His power is most evident. Second Corinthians 12:9 reminds us of a powerful truth from the Lord: "My grace is sufficient for you, for my power is made perfect in weakness." God's grace meets us in our shortcomings, and His power is magnified when we surrender our inadequacies to Him.

In those moments when the weight of the task feels too heavy, God covers you with His abundant grace. He invites you to rest in your weakness and watch Him take over in incredible ways. When others see your reliance on God, they'll see His power at work too. So if you feel weak today, embrace it. His grace is enough, and His power shines brightest in your need.

"Being a mother is learning about strengths you didn't know you had."[6]

—Linda Wooten

Remember This

Some of your most effective moments as a mother will be when you're operating outside of your strengths. As you rely on God, His power will be made perfect through your weakness.

When Jealousy Creeps In

A tranquil heart gives life to the flesh,
but envy makes the bones rot.

Proverbs 14:30 (ESV)

Maybe you've felt that familiar pang. You're scrolling through social media when suddenly your confidence falters and your joy evaporates. You know they're mommas just like you—proud of their babies, their husbands, or a picture-worthy outing—but that doesn't stop the feeling gnawing at the pit of your stomach like a flesh-eating virus. And just like that, jealousy rears its ugly head.

You may wonder: *Is her life better than mine? Is she*

a more patient, kind, or cool mom than I am? Are her kids turning out better than mine? Does she have more friends?

Why is it that we turn to social media to feel a sense of worth? We're all just trying to survive motherhood with dignity and humor. And yet, it's so tempting to compare ourselves and judge our performance on whose pictures are prettier. The work of motherhood is beautiful but often invisible. You may see other moms doing great things and wonder if anyone notices *your* daily, unseen victories. That's when envy can strike.

Proverbs tells us that a tranquil heart—one rooted in contentment—gives life to the flesh, while envy rots the bones. Peace doesn't come from having what others have but from knowing who you are in Christ. God has given you everything you need for the task of being a mom. Focus on His faithfulness. Allow the truth that you are seen, loved, and equipped to settle your heart. Even if another mom's highlight reel flashes before your eyes, you are free to respond with genuine happiness for her. If you can't, consider taking a break from social media.

Ask God to replace envy with peace. Cultivate gratitude for where He's placed you and be willing to be happy for another mom in the trenches.

"The more you compare,

the less you appreciate what's yours."

—Unknown

Remember This . . .

God sees your daily faithfulness. To gain a tranquil heart, focus on what He's provided and how He's equipped you.

Taking Every Opportunity

Love the L*ORD your God with all your heart and with all your soul and with all your strength. These commandments that I give you today are to be on your hearts. Impress them on your children. Talk about them when you sit at home and when you walk along the road, when you lie down and when you get up.*

DEUTERONOMY 6:5–7

We live in an instant world—mobile coffee orders, information at our fingertips, drive-through everything, and free overnight shipping. Such luxuries make us feel like we can have everything *now* and shouldn't have to wait.

Sometimes we may adopt this same thinking with our kids. We want to see instant results from our parenting. When they kick their shoes off in the middle of the floor two days (or even weeks) in a row, it's aggravating. When they've been told not to fight, and yet the yells echo through the house, it's infuriating. And when they fall into the same sinful pitfalls we've experienced, it's heartbreaking.

The truth is, raising children who embrace God's truth and His ways isn't an instant process. God's parenting instructions to His people, the Israelites, emphasized impressing His truth and commands on their children through many little interactions day after day. He encouraged them to first love Him with their whole hearts and then to impress His Word on the hearts of their children. Our own love for God fuels the spiritual conversations we have with our kids.

To impress God's commandments on our kids, we must talk with them daily about who God is and what He says. Some of the best conversations occur in the most mundane moments—at the breakfast table, in the car, watching TV together, or just before turning off the lights at night.

Raising Jesus-followers doesn't happen overnight. Spiritual growth is a process for both us and our kids. As we take advantage of the everyday opportunities to teach our children about God, we can trust that He will bless our efforts.

"Fathers and mothers are the most natural agents for God to use in the salvation of their children."[7]

—Charles Spurgeon

Remember This

Raising the next generation of Christ-followers is a process of impressing His truth on our children through many daily interactions driven by our own love for God.

Finding Balance

Come to me, all you who are weary and burdened, and I will give you rest. Take my yoke upon you and learn from me, for I am gentle and humble in heart, and you will find rest for your souls. For my yoke is easy and my burden is light.

Matthew 11:28–30

The work of motherhood—especially in the early years—can feel like an endless loop of messes, meals, and meltdowns. Whether you stay at home with your little ones or work outside the home, making time for rest, reflection, and prayer can feel impossible.

In her book *Look What You've Done,* CCM artist Tasha Layton describes a season where she felt overworked and overwhelmed: "I was feeling a lot of pressure because

I had to leave my kids behind more often than I wanted," she writes. "I wanted to take advantage of doors opening but not at the expense of my job as a mom."[8]

A friend encouraged her to protect her priorities and her calling. Only she could determine the best use of her time and energy. Some of that time would be spent doing the work of wiping sticky hands, sweeping up Cheerios, kissing boo-boos, and dropping into bed exhausted at the end of the day. But God also invited her to write, sing, and perform for His glory. Living out her full calling required her to balance priorities, accept help, and be intentional about rest.

The sacred work of motherhood stretches us to our limits emotionally, mentally, and spiritually, but Jesus offers us rest. He invites us to learn from Him. It's okay to feel inadequate. God asks for faithfulness not perfection. As you share His yoke, Jesus helps you "learn the unforced rhythms of grace" (Matt. 11:28–30 MSG). As a bonus, when we relax in God's care, we model rest for our children.

If you are in a tiring season where balance feels elusive, rest in Jesus. Don't be afraid to accept help. And remember: You are never alone.

"Running errands and taking care of my home are important tasks. . . . But there's no shame in asking for help when I have something more pressing or of eternal value to do."[9]

—Tasha Layton

Remember This

In the busyness of motherhood, Jesus offers us rest and helps us prioritize what matters most. Rest is part of His good plan and helps us more fully live out the purposes He has for us.

Being an Original

But in fact God has placed the parts in the body, every one of them, just as he wanted them to be. If they were all one part, where would the body be? As it is, there are many parts, but one body.

1 Corinthians 12:18–20

If you ever visit a kindergarten classroom, you'll quickly realize how different children can be. Some pay careful attention to the task at hand. Others chat with their neighbors. Still others notice the needs of the children around them and deliver a pencil or glue stick to a student in need. Each child is unique with different personalities, preferences, strengths, and weaknesses.

It's easy to look at children and see how God made each one unique, but sometimes we forget to apply that same knowledge to ourselves. We compare ourselves when we see another mom doing things differently—or seemingly better—than we do. Some moms are task-oriented, crushing their daily to-do lists. Others create amazing art projects for their children or take them to the park every day. Still others excel at cooking healthy meals for their children or leading deep, spiritual conversations.

Just as children possess unique characteristics, so do their mothers. And it's a relief to realize we don't all have to fit the same mold. In 1 Corinthians 12, Paul describes us as parts of one body. Each part is distinctive, but the parts all need each other to function properly: "The eye cannot say to the hand, 'I don't need you!' And the head cannot say to the feet, 'I don't need you!' On the contrary, those parts of the body that seem to be weaker are indispensable" (vv. 21–22).

As Christian moms, we're all in this together. Our differences are intentional because, like parts of the body, we're designed to work together. When we feel like the weaker parts, Scripture reminds us that we are *indispensable.* God has placed you exactly where He wants you to be. You don't have to be like other moms. You're free to be the mom He created you to be.

"Live outside the box you may have put around your life. Don't be afraid to look different from society's norm. Have courage to step out and take hold of the dream God has placed in your heart and trust Him."[10]

—Helen Smallbone

Remember This

God has designed you with unique characteristics to bless your children and has placed you where you are meant to be.

Raising Jesus-followers doesn't happen overnight. Spiritual growth is a process for both us and our kids.

13

Grace in the Mom Guilt

If we confess our sins, he is faithful
and just and will forgive us our sins
and purify us from all unrighteousness.

1 John 1:9

Mom guilt takes many forms. Sometimes we may feel like we're not giving our children all the right life experiences. Other times, we may obsess over feeding them the right foods or modeling consistent Christian character. And then there are the times when the guilt is thick as molasses because we've *really* blown it.

Maybe you lost your temper and screamed at your kids. Perhaps you misjudged a situation and issued a severe punishment that didn't fit the crime. Maybe you unleashed a critical comment that hurt your child's confidence. Moms blow it at times, but our failure does not surprise God.

Scripture offers this hope in Proverbs 24:16: "For though the righteous fall seven times, they rise again, but the wicked stumble when calamity strikes." The righteous *will* fall repeatedly . . . but they will rise again. As moms, we need this reminder: When we fall, we get back up.

Sometimes that looks like going to our child and asking for forgiveness for a wrong we've committed. Other times it's quickly apologizing for a harsh word or unfair reaction. It's never too late to repair or reconcile the relationship with our child. God promises He will help us (2 Cor. 5:18).

Keep in mind that God's mercies are new every morning (Lam. 3:23). He offers us His grace and an unlimited number of do-overs through Jesus Christ. As we confess our sins and receive His forgiveness, we model for our kids how to deal with sin and make things right. We show them that when they fall, they can rise again. That is the power of imperfect moms.

"God's perfect grace is the foundation
that keeps us standing firm as mothers."[11]

—Rachael Elmore

Remember This—

When we blow it as moms, we can receive God's forgiveness and make things right with those we've hurt.

Encouraging Your Child's Calling

And let us consider how we may spur one another on toward love and good deeds.

Hebrews 10:24

One of the joys of motherhood is watching our children begin to embrace their God-given passions and gifts. We marvel as our sons excel in basketball or learn to play piano concertos. We burst with pride when our daughters perform in the school play or head off on a mission trip. We celebrate as our kids achieve milestones, get their first jobs, and learn to drive.

Growing up as pastor's kids, the siblings in

CAIN—Taylor, Madison, and Logan—had a unique opportunity to hone their musical gifts and performance abilities. Madison recalls her parents would allow her and her siblings to "test out" their latest inspirations on the church congregation. Each time the Cain children asked to bring a song, dance, or "word" from the stage, their parents agreed.

"I imagine the church members must have rolled their eyes when, Sunday after Sunday, they had to sit through the Cain children talent show before they could hear a good sermon," she writes in *We're So Blessed.* But she now sees how God used those experiences to prepare the siblings for their future music ministry. "As part of our band CAIN, we are constantly on a stage, 'giving a word' and making up a song and dance."[12]

As moms, we can look for the seeds God has planted in our children's hearts and create opportunities for them to grow. Consider what unique connections and opportunities you have as a family that can serve to cultivate your child's passions and spiritual gifts. God already knows exactly who your children are going to be. As their mom, cooperate with the Spirit to provide opportunities for them to practice their passions.

"Parents, look at your children. Who they'll become one day, the future God has for them, is already inside of them right now! You have the precious opportunity to use what you have to nurture that gifting." [13]

—Madison Cain Johnson

Remember This

God has given your children gifts and passions. Look for ways to nurture and encourage their unique designs.

Superpowers

I praise you because I am fearfully and wonderfully made; your works are wonderful, I know that full well.

Psalm 139:14

When singer-songwriter Rachael Lampa found out she was going to have a baby with Down syndrome, she was in the middle of a tour rehearsal and thought she was simply going to hear back about the sex of the baby.

"I hung up the phone, and before my default setting of worry had a chance to take the stage, I felt a bubble of peace around me and have felt it ever since," she says. That October, Rachael, her husband, Brendan, and their oldest son, Jackson, welcomed baby Leo. Despite the typical momma worries she had for her special little guy, Rachael says she felt the Lord holding her—even through a difficult pregnancy and emergency C-section.

"Leo is a comforter," she says, "and he was showing me that from day one. I knew I was being carried as I carried him." Leo is now a joyful toddler and the inspiration behind Rachael's song "Superpowers," which she released on World Down Syndrome Day, March 21, 2025. She says Leo is "part of something really holy and beautiful that God has offered to me and my family—to walk with someone who has such light and such a gift to bring to the world." [14]

Though her life was turned upside down with Leo's diagnosis, Rachael discovered that God was bigger than her fears and infinitely worthy of her trust. He had a beautiful plan far beyond what she could have imagined.

*"Leo is everything good and right in this world . . .
inside and out . . . there's nothing down about him. . . .
He's our little compass reminding us that we don't have to
keep up with the speed of the world if we don't want to.
That there is a richness in slowing down."*[15]

—Rachael Lampa

Remember This

Our children are fearfully and wonderfully made by God. Each one is a gift that He uses to enrich our lives and show us more of His character.

No More Shoulds

"Not by might nor by power,
but by my Spirit," says the Lord Almighty.
ZECHARIAH 4:6

Are you the kind of mom who thrives on planning, preparation, and structure? You make sure to keep the house running, the calendar organized, and meals on the table. This is great when life goes as planned. But once a child gets sick, a nap gets missed, or your toddler melts down in the middle of the store, suddenly that sense of control slips through your fingers like baby powder.

Motherhood has a way of exposing our limits. And when life begins to feel chaotic, we may turn inward and begin to pile on the "I shoulds."

- I should have more patience.
- I should be doing my devotions every day.
- I should be a better mom.
- I should make more time to pray.

In our hearts, we long to do what's best for our kids. We want to love our families well and honor God. But the truth is God didn't intend for us to do this job out of sheer effort or determination.

In Zechariah 4:6, the Lord reminded Zerubbabel that the temple would not be rebuilt by human strength but by His Spirit. God gives us a similar message. We don't carry our calling alone. God's Spirit is with us in the chaos, in the fatigue, and in the moments of self-doubt and self-condemnation.

When we shift our eyes from our weakness to His sufficiency, the pressure of "I should" begins to fade. God doesn't ask you to do this important work in your own strength; He invites you to surrender control to Him. His Spirit is at work in you, accomplishing what your power and might never could.

"Whether I'm a 'good' mom or disappoint myself all day long, He loves me in Christ. In a season full of unknowns and variables, it is so comforting to have this truth to hold on to." [16]

—Rachel Denison

Remember This

You don't have to live in the guilt-inducing world of "I shoulds." God calls you to lay aside your own might and determination and rely on His Spirit to give you what you need.

17

Spirit-Led Mothering

For those who are led
by the Spirit of God
are the children of God.

ROMANS 8:14

We have a powerful Helper in our assignment as mothers. Scripture reminds us that the Holy Spirit is constantly with us, guiding us and giving us wisdom. He helps us see opportunities to participate in His work every day. At times, He even offers us protection. A few years ago, Naomi Raine, award-winning singer-songwriter and mom of three, discovered this truth firsthand.

Naomi had been praying daily, asking the Holy Spirit to teach her how to hear His voice and be led by Him. One afternoon, she was walking past the stairs when she noticed a piece of paper that had fallen from her son Kayden's bag.

She says, "Immediately I felt frustrated and thought, *He's going to pick that up when he gets home. I'm not his maid, and he needs to learn responsibility.*

"In that moment, I felt the Holy Spirit nudge me: *Pick it up.*

"I pushed back: *No—he needs to learn to listen when I tell him to clean up after himself!*"

Not long after her conversation with God, Naomi heard a loud thud followed by crying. Her younger son, Savion, had slipped on the paper and hit his head on the step.

"Thank God he was okay," she says. "But as I held him close, comforting him, I heard the Lord whisper: *Do you see what it looks like to learn your lesson the hard way? Are YOU going to listen to Me?* In that moment, it hit me—my obedience to the Holy Spirit isn't just about me. It protects my children. If I let my own reasoning override His voice, it can cause unnecessary harm."

Galatians 5:25 urges us, "Since we live by the Spirit, let us keep in step with the Spirit." The benefits of yielding to the Spirit's prompting are many—both for mother and child. Learning to move with the Spirit is a lifelong process, but as His child, you don't have to overthink every step—simply listen and follow His lead.

"His wisdom is always greater than mine,
and His instruction is never random.
It's always meant to cover, protect, and guide us."
—Naomi Raine

Remember This

The Holy Spirit guides us and gives us wisdom in our roles as mothers. As we keep in step with the Spirit, we will reap benefits for both ourselves and our children.

Cultivating Gratitude

I will extol the Lord at all times;
his praise will always be on my lips.
I will glory in the Lord;
let the afflicted hear and rejoice.
Glorify the Lord with me;
let us exalt his name together.

Psalm 34:1–3

Cultivating an attitude of gratitude can be a challenge. In 1 Thessalonians 5:18, Paul encourages us to, "give thanks in all circumstances; for this is God's will for you in Christ Jesus." This can be difficult when the children are fighting or when we spend an hour cooking dinner only to have everyone complain. Most of us would prefer life to run smoothly—with plenty of sleep, everyone getting along, and a perpetually clean house. Unfortunately, that's not typically how life goes.

It's interesting that Paul didn't say, "Give thanks in happy circumstances" or "Be grateful when everything is going your way." Instead, he said that God's will is for us to give thanks in *all* circumstances (something he had personal experience with, by the way). We can give thanks when the family gathers and there is laughter and joy, *and* we can give thanks when the car breaks down on the way to school pickup. Whatever life throws at us, we can choose to praise.

As a mom, you can model an attitude of gratitude that is infectious. In her book *Believe for It*, CeCe Winans recounts a humorous story from when her kids were young. One morning while CeCe was out of town, her children made a video of part of their day.

"As they climbed into the car to go to school," she says, "Ashley, pretending to be me, raised her hand and said, 'Oh God, we bless Your name.'

"'God, You are so good!' Alvin III chimed in.

"I smiled, both at their amusing impersonation of

their mother and at the fact that they had picked up on my inclination to praise."[17]

The habit of voicing our thanks to God impacts our children and makes our hearts light (Ps. 28:7). At times, we may have to get creative to turn a situation into an opportunity to praise, but when we do, we become more aware of God's loving presence in our lives.

"As a girl, I witnessed the power of praise firsthand. Rain or shine, my dad was always praising Jesus. . . . My mother also kept praise on her lips, though she was less boisterous about it. . . . I never doubted how my mom or dad felt about the Lord or how deeply they trusted Him."[18]

—CeCe Winans

Remember This

As we make gratitude and thankfulness a way of life, we will influence our children to become more aware of God's greatness and work in our lives.

God already knows exactly who your children are going to be.

Peace in Motherhood

Do not be anxious about anything,
but in every situation, by prayer and petition,
with thanksgiving, present your requests to God.
And the peace of God, which transcends
all understanding, will guard your hearts
and your minds in Christ Jesus.

Philippians 4:6–7

Have you ever lain awake at night with the cares of the day racing through your mind? You may wonder how you can possibly solve the problems you face. Financial stresses, decisions about your children's future, health concerns, and marriage problems can feel overpowering and impossible to solve.

It's been said, "Worry is like a rocking chair; it gives you something to do but never gets you anywhere." When we get stuck in the rocking chair of worry, we become focused on our problems instead of God's provision.

When we're weighed down by worry, God reminds us that peace doesn't come from figuring everything out but from releasing our worries to Him. That's difficult to do. Moms are solvers, and we want everything to be right in our own lives and in the lives of those we love. In Philippians, Paul offers a simple but powerful invitation: *Pray about everything*—not just the "big stuff," but every minor care weighing on your heart. And give thanks to God because gratitude shifts our perspective. When we thank God for His faithfulness to us in the past, our trust deepens for the future.

Our problems likely won't disappear overnight, but God promises us His supernatural peace in the midst of them. We don't experience this peace because our circumstances are perfect, but because our focus has shifted from the problem to the Provider.

God never asked you to carry your burdens alone. The next time anxiety creeps in, pray about it! Don't leave anything out. Then thank Him for your children, His daily provision, and His faithful presence in your life. As you do, notice how His peace settles over your soul.

"All the peace and favour of the world cannot calm a troubled heart; but where this peace is which Christ gives, all the trouble and disquiet of the world cannot disturb it."

—Robert Leighton

Remember This

Go to God in prayer in every situation with honest requests and a thankful heart. You may not be able to fix every problem, but you know the One who can.

20

Embracing Your Kids

Accept one another, then, just as Christ accepted you, in order to bring praise to God.

Romans 15:7

Some days, motherhood pushes us to the edge. We love our children deeply, but there are moments when we may struggle to accept them as they are. One child's endless questions wear on your nerves. Your reserved or sensitive child makes you worry about his ability to connect. Another's loudness in public embarrasses you.

Your children are not you. That means they won't think the way you do or make the same choices (they wouldn't even if they had your maturity). And while that may cause frustration and make it hard to connect at times, the way they express their individuality is by divine design.

The Lord created your children with unique personalities, attributes, and abilities to build His kingdom. Romans tells us to accept each other—including our children—just as Christ accepts us. That's a tall order. Acceptance isn't approval of every behavior but the choice to embrace who our child is becoming.

Our job as moms isn't to mold our children into smaller versions of ourselves but to love them and guide them to become the people God made them to be. That kind of acceptance brings Him glory. It teaches our kids that their worth isn't tied to perfection or performance but is rooted in being fully known and fully loved.

We won't always get it right, which is why we lean on Jesus—who not only accepts our children but also accepts us. Ask Him for eyes to see your child through His lens. As your children grow, may you be the one who faithfully cheers them on to walk boldly in the unique calling God has placed on their lives.

"A mother is the truest friend we have,
when trials heavy and sudden, fall upon us . . .
still will she cling to us, and endeavor by her kind
precepts and counsels to dissipate the clouds of darkness,
and cause peace to return to our hearts."[19]

—Washington Irving

Remember This

God gives us the ability to accept our children the way Christ accepts us. When we allow our kids to be who they are, it brings praise to God for His workmanship.

Important Work

Children are a heritage from the L*ORD*,
offspring a reward from him.
Like arrows in the hands of a warrior are
children born in one's youth. Blessed is the
man whose quiver is full of them.

Psalm 127:3–5

In the busy, everyday moments of motherhood, we may feel like our work doesn't matter much. But Scripture reveals that couldn't be further from the truth! We're not just raising children—we're shaping warriors for the kingdom. And our homes are the training ground. We don't just provide for our children's physical needs—although that is a key part of being a mom—but we also nurture hearts, souls, and minds.

Being a mom is a privilege! We get to take an active role in shaping their beliefs and character as we invite them to follow us as we follow Christ. Our children learn about Jesus's love as they watch *us* love others. They learn courage as they see *us* step out in faith and stand for what is right. They learn grace as they watch *us* offer it, even when it's difficult. They are watching us, learning how to follow Jesus and live out faith.

This world is dark and desperate for truth and God's love. Heartbreaking news stories fill our feeds daily, and our own homes and families are not immune to brokenness and tragedy. Scripture encourages us, reminding us our battle is not of a physical nature but "against the powers of this dark world and against the spiritual forces of evil in the heavenly realms" (Eph. 6:12). One day our children will stand in this battle as adults. What kind of arrows will they be—dull and aimless or sharp and ready?

As mothers, we can prepare them by teaching them the truth. We can sharpen them by modeling grace, humility, and a strong work ethic. We can shape their aim through our faithful prayers and loving presence. Don't ever underestimate the value of your labor. One day we'll release our arrows, and they will launch into the world carrying Jesus with them.

"The influence of a mother upon the lives of her children cannot be measured. They know and absorb her example and attitudes when it comes to questions of honesty, temperance, kindness, and industry."[20]

—Billy Graham

Remember This

Your daily efforts as a mom make a difference. As you point your kids to Jesus, you prepare them to be godly warriors for the kingdom.

Don't Give Up

Let us not become weary in doing good,
for at the proper time we will reap
a harvest if we do not give up.

Galatians 6:9

Motherhood requires a heavy investment. We don't always see the fruit of the sacrifices made, conversations had, or prayers lifted.

CeCe Winans says that when her children were teens, she learned she could not only pray about her concerns for them but also thank God for His good plans for their lives. She would thank God that her daughter was a woman of valor and godly character. Whether her daughter exhibited those characteristics or not, CeCe prayed them, knowing her prayers were in accordance with God's will.

In her book *Believe for It,* she talks about a surprising interaction she had with her teenage son, Alvin.

> "As he was growing into a young man, my son had become a person I didn't fully understand or even recognize. . . . During an argument, I blurted out, 'Alvin, you are a mighty man of God!'
>
> "He stopped arguing and looked at my quizzically. 'You don't even believe that yourself,' he said.
>
> "And he was right! But I didn't let him know that. My words had caught my son's attention. He had heard my proclamation of his godly character." [21]

Before he would walk in that calling, Alvin still had some things to wrestle through, CeCe says. However, eventually he embraced it, and today he is a pastor who is fully sold out to the Lord.

Regardless of your child's present behavior, you can point them toward Christ instead of backing away from them. As you thank Him for His righteous plans for your child, you can trust that you are planting seeds that will one day bear fruit.

"When people ask me what I did to have strong relationships with my grown children, I say, 'I fought for it.' It wasn't always easy."[22]

—CeCe Winans

Remember This

God promises we will reap a harvest if we do not give up. He hears our prayers and answers them. Thank God in advance for making the seeds of godliness grow in your child's life.

Valuable Mistakes

And we know that in all things God works for the good of those who love him, who have been called according to his purpose.

Romans 8:28

When our kids are young, caring for their needs feels uncomplicated for the most part. We feed them, clothe them, keep them away from danger, and brush away their tears. As they get older, the landscape can suddenly shift from manageable to feeling like an emotional minefield.

As the mom of two teens, singer Naomi Raine understands this dynamic. In her opinion, allowing her children to make their own choices is one of the most challenging parts of motherhood. "You must discern when to weigh in and when to keep quiet," she says. "You have to trust that God is going to work everything together for good even when you don't love their decisions."

When we see our children making questionable decisions, we have options. We can:

> **Pray.** God invites us to bring our toughest parenting challenges to Him, and He will give us wisdom and act for our good and His glory.
>
> **Talk.** We can gently approach our children when we notice them heading in a concerning direction. Ask questions to get to the heart of the matter. Try reading Proverbs together to highlight the consequences of unwise choices and the blessings that come from good decisions.
>
> **Love.** When poor decisions lead to consequences, we can use the experience as a teachable moment while still affirming our love for them and reminding them of God's mercy.

"I want to be there for my kids and be a soft landing when their poor decisions haven't panned out well," Naomi says. "It's hard to watch them get hurt, but it's life."

As our children get older, they need us more than ever. They need our guidance—even when they pretend they don't. They need our prayers and our love. As they get tossed around by the storms of life, moms can reframe disappointments and failures as opportunities for God to show His power by working all things together for good.

"Motherhood isn't a sprint; it's a marathon. Each day is the first attempt you've made at that day. So learn from the days before and keep going! You are the only mother your children will have, and God chose you. Don't give up; you can do it!"

—Naomi Raine

Remember This

Your child's faulty decisions provide opportunities to offer guidance, speak truth, and express love.

Power in Imperfection

That is why, for Christ's sake, I delight in weaknesses, in insults, in hardships, in persecutions, in difficulties. For when I am weak, then I am strong.

2 Corinthians 12:10

Have you ever felt like a failure as a mom? Caring for our children's physical, emotional, and spiritual needs presents many opportunities to fall short. And yet culture and social media sell the lie that it's possible to be the perfect mom. So we put pressure on ourselves to succeed in every area. We may prioritize providing healthy meals, keeping the house in order, making sure our kids are consistently at church, or providing them with a variety of experiences and social opportunities.

In recent years, research has revealed the extreme "mental load" mothers endure. The mental load is the unseen work of running a household and managing a family. One publication described it as "the never-ending, behind-the-scenes mental gymnastics required for everything to get done."[23] Maybe you can relate. And the more we pile on, the more we feel like we're not doing anything well. Then comes the mom guilt.

God doesn't want us to live in that place. He wants us to live empowered by His Spirit. When the Apostle Paul faced a low time in his ministry, he described it as a thorn in his flesh—an aggravation sent to keep him from becoming conceited. Nothing humbles you like being a mom. The work of motherhood is a constant reminder of our weaknesses.

Ultimately, Paul accepted that the "thorn" was the very thing God was using to display His power (2 Cor. 12:7). It's amazing to realize that when we feel at our worst, God exhibits His best. His greatest work takes place through our imperfection. It's freeing to know we don't have to be perfect. Instead, we can faithfully do our best and trust that God is using us powerfully despite our weaknesses.

"There's no way to be a perfect mother and a million ways to be a good one."

—Jill Churchill

Remember This

Perfection in motherhood is a myth. God shows His power as you rely on Him for strength.

the Lord created your children with unique personalities, attributes, and abilities to build His kingdom.

Battling Burnout

Are you tired? Worn out?
Burned out on religion? Come to me.
Get away with me and you'll recover your life.
I'll show you how to take a real rest.
Walk with me and work with me—
watch how I do it. Learn the unforced
rhythms of grace. I won't lay anything heavy
or ill-fitting on you. Keep company with me
and you'll learn to live freely and lightly.

Matthew 11:28–30 (MSG)

Singer Hope Darst, mom of two teenage daughters, says burnout is real. She admits that she has struggled with the question, "How do I do it all?" As a working mom with a full schedule and a wife to a husband who runs several businesses, the "Mighty Name of Jesus" singer also juggles her daughters' busy schedules and the family's commitments serving in the local church.

"The pressure to 'do it all' is a constant battle," she says. "I can't do it in my own strength or wisdom, but I can lean in and partner with the Holy Spirit. My job isn't to keep it all together; it's to keep close company with Jesus.

"The mission of motherhood," Hope says, is "the same as everything we do in our lives—to reflect the image and glory of Jesus and be faithful servants." When we focus on the core aspects of following Jesus, it takes the pressure off. "My true calling is to follow Jesus and leave my kids knowing that following Him is the best decision they could ever make."

"God has created mothers to be incredible leaders, creative thinkers, helpers, nurturers and the CEOs of their homes and families while doing it filled with the power and wisdom of the Lord and the guidance of the Holy Spirit."

—Hope Darst

Remember This

When burnout hits, go back to the basics: Keep company with Jesus and receive His grace and rest.

A Bigger Purpose

Very truly I tell you, unless a kernel of wheat falls to the ground and dies, it remains only a single seed. But if it dies, it produces many seeds.

John 12:24

The years of caring for young children can feel monotonous and never-ending. Madison Cain Johnson of CAIN understands this well. "I thrive on novelty and life being an adventure," she says. "So when I'm doing the same things day after day, it's hard for me to stay focused."

As you care for your children, you can be confident that Jesus is by your side, lightening the load as you fold the laundry, wipe little noses, stir the macaroni noodles, and pick up the toys (again). Much of the work you do in the early years is unseen and uncelebrated, but that doesn't mean it's unimportant.

Madison points to the words of John 12:24, which speak of a kernel of wheat dying so it may produce many seeds. "There's this illusion when you're doing hard things that you would be happier without the work of motherhood," she says. "But everyone suffers hard things in life, and as a mom, you can know your suffering has a greater purpose."

Moms put in long days, but the years of mothering young children are fleeting (even when it feels like they'll never end). In every mundane task, God sees you. He will bless your sacrifice, and your labor in Him is never in vain.

"My presence is a comfort to my children. Whether I feel like I've been a good mom or a bad mom that day, just me being near is a comfort to them. I think that's a gift."

—Madison Cain Johnson

Remember This

Your unseen moments of caring for your children are seen by God. Each sacrifice and act of service has a greater purpose.

Promises for Weary Moms

For no matter how many promises God has made, they are 'Yes' in Christ.

2 CORINTHIANS 1:20

Motherhood is filled with holy moments—first steps, sticky kisses, and bedtime prayers. It's also filled with exhaustion, messes, and moments of deep self-doubt. Amid sleepless nights, toddler tantrums, and endless to-do lists, it's easy to wonder: Do God's promises really apply to this season?

The answer is a resounding yes! Scripture is filled with promises of hope and help that apply to moms. We know them: God is with us. He is our helper. We are more than conquerors. But when your baby won't sleep, the whole family gets the stomach flu, and you've lost it with your hormonal teen for the third time that day, those promises can feel far away—or like they're meant for someone stronger and more equipped.

Yet God's Word tells us that every promise of God finds its yes in Jesus. That means those truths are just as real in the trenches of motherhood as they are sitting in the most prestigious seminary. His promises are firm. Jesus offers rest, even when it doesn't come in the form of a full night's sleep. He offers peace when worries flood your mind. His promises don't depend on your feelings or your performance but are rooted in His unchanging character. Though your season may shift, His faithfulness never changes.

When your soul feels weary, go back to God's promises. Speak them over your home. Claim them for your family. Hide them in your heart. His promises are the common thread in your journey through this life. God's yes to you stands firm today, tomorrow, and forever.

"Motherhood is a million little moments that God weaves together with grace, redemption, laughter, tears, and most of all love. Such a gift."[24]

—Lysa TerKeurst

Remember This

God's promises are true in this season. Cling to His Word and remember His grace is enough for today.

28

Don't Do It Alone

Carry each other's burdens, and in this way you will fulfill the law of Christ.

Galatians 6:2

Many of us embark on the journey of motherhood feeling like we have to do everything on our own. Maybe we want to prove we can handle it. Perhaps we're afraid to ask for help. But at some point, we realize the truth: We need other moms who can walk by our sides and who have gone before us. We need them to remind us that we all share similar struggles.

Cultivating community requires time and effort. Sometimes it's messy and inconvenient. It means taking the baby along to Bible study or calling a friend for prayer or practical help on a hard day. But as we push through and connect with other women, we learn that we're not alone. We discover that God designed us to carry one another's burdens and love each other deeply.

In a fast-paced world, deep friendships can be hard to find. But we were never meant to take this motherhood journey alone. God created us for connection—to lean on one another and share the load. For this to happen, we must let go of pride and be willing to reach out. Asking for help—and receiving it—requires humility. But that's exactly where He wants us—in relationship.

If you feel alone today, reach out. Ask for prayer. Join a Bible study. Be honest. Then watch God meet your needs through the hands and hearts of His people.

"God has given us two hands—one to receive with and the other to give with. We are not cisterns made for hoarding; we are channels made for sharing."

—Billy Graham

Remember This

You don't have to carry your burdens by yourself. God designed you to be interconnected with other women who can share the load.

Trust and Obey

Obey me, and I will be your God and you will be my people. Walk in obedience to all I command you, that it may go well with you.

Jeremiah 7:23

In her book *It's Never Wrong to Do the Right Thing*, singer-songwriter Nicole C. Mullen recalls a piece of parenting advice she heard from her mom when her kids were young: "Teach your children to heed your voice the first time, because the second time could cost them their lives. If you can train them to respond in obedience first, you will be afforded the pleasure of explanation later."[25]

Nicole, who applied this advice to her parenting, recalls a situation in which the importance of its truth was shown. When her youngest son was eleven, the family had temporarily moved into a new home. As they were moving in, her preteen felt confident enough to carry her large desktop computer up a flight of stairs. Nicole wasn't so sure and told him to be careful. "My single mom budget was on high alert, and yet I did my best to remain calm and encouraging," she writes.[26]

Halfway up the stairs, he stumbled and dropped the computer, which contained important music files, notes, photos, and programs. Resisting the urge to yell, Nicole says she realized there was more at stake than broken hardware. "I was still shaping clay, and he was only eleven. He had been through enough."[27]

Instead of yelling, she said, "Freeze"—and her son did. "His quick obedience gave me time to explain that there were shards of glass beneath his bare feet. Had he taken another step, or been slow to obey, it would have hurt him. My voice of alarm was not to scare or shame him but for his protection."[28]

God works with us in the same way, Nicole says. As we obey, He offers us protection, blessing, and grace for our mistakes. Not only can we teach our children to obey quickly, we can also model it by submitting to our heavenly Father.

"Sometimes His voice is still and small.
Other times it is loud and urgent.
And yet, regardless of the volume,
the aim is for us to listen and obey right away."[29]

—Nicole C. Mullen

Remember This

God asks us to obey Him for our good and our protection. We can pass on this important truth to our children as we teach them immediate obedience.

The Cross of Motherhood

Then Jesus said to his disciples, "Whoever wants to be my disciple must deny themselves and take up their cross and follow me."

MATTHEW 16:24

Mothering is a study in intense sacrifice and self-denial. There are moments of deep joy, but there are also times of confusion, heartache, and exhaustion. As our children grow into their teen years, we may find ourselves biting our tongues and praying harder than ever before. In this space, Jesus's words take on new significance: "Whoever wants to be my disciple must deny themselves and take up their cross and follow me."

Sometimes that cross is showing love when our teen is disrespectful and choosing patience when every part of us wants to react in frustration. Other times, it's setting boundaries that aren't popular or remaining faithful in prayer when it feels like nothing is changing.

Obedience to Christ as a mother isn't always glamorous. Many times it means denying ourselves the comfort of being understood or appreciated. It might require sacrificing our own plans to show up for our children again and again—even when they push us away.

The good news is that within these sacrifices, Jesus is shaping us to be more like Him. Each act of faith, no matter how small, draws us closer to His Presence. And the peace that follows surrender is real. God sees your quiet faithfulness, Mom, and your obedience in this season matters greatly.

What cross is Jesus asking you to carry today? Where do you sense Him inviting you to trust and obey? Take a moment to yield your heart to Him once again.

"I always wanted to be a hero—to sacrifice my life in a big way one time—and yet, God has required my sacrifice to be thousands of days, over many years, with one more kiss, one more story, one more meal."[30]

—Sally Clarkson

Remember This

God sees your sacrifice and is using it to transform you into the image of Christ. Each act of surrender and self-denial allows you to follow Him more closely.

Watch God
meet your needs
through the
hands and hearts
of His people.

Asking for Wisdom

If any of you lacks wisdom, you should ask God, who gives generously to all without finding fault, and it will be given to you.

James 1:5

Motherhood is full of moments that leave us wondering what to do next—sleepless nights with a colicky baby, late-night conversations with an emotional teen, dozens of weekly decisions about school, work, and family balance. With so much riding on our choices, it's easy to feel overwhelmed and underqualified.

But God offers us a lifeline: He invites us to ask Him for wisdom, and He will give it generously, without finding fault. Isn't that a beautiful promise? God doesn't shame us for not knowing what to do. He doesn't sigh when we come to Him yet again. Instead, He welcomes our questions and confusion—even our desperation—and He gives wisdom freely.

In a dream, God offered King Solomon anything he desired. The king's request is recorded in 1 Kings 3:9: "So give your servant a discerning heart to govern your people and to distinguish between right and wrong." The Lord was pleased with this request and granted Solomon immense wisdom and knowledge along with riches and honor. God loves when we ask Him for wisdom to govern "our people"—the precious lives He's entrusted to us.

While seeking advice online or from a wise friend may be our first inclination, God tells us we can come to Him directly! He knows your child and your situation better than anyone. He also sees your heart and knows exactly what wisdom you need.

So whether you're facing a meltdown at the breakfast table or making a life-changing decision for your family, stop and ask God for wisdom. You don't have to parent alone.

She speaks with wisdom, and
faithful instruction is on her tongue.

—Proverbs 31:26

Remember this

God promises to give you wisdom when you ask. He knows your heart and what is best for your family.

Patience in the Process

Let us not become weary in doing good,
for at the proper time we will reap a harvest
if we do not give up.

Galatians 6:9

Motherhood is made up of long days and many unseen tasks. Sometimes the journey feels like planting seeds you can't always see. You pour out love and teach truth, wondering if any of it is taking root. But God's Word reminds us: Don't give up!

Just as a farmer doesn't see fruit the day after planting, the work we do in our homes takes time to produce a harvest. When we practice patience in the process, we trust that God is growing something beautiful even when we don't see the results. You may feel weary or like you're not doing enough, but when your heart is set on doing good for your children—by loving, serving, correcting, and encouraging them—God promises that your labor is not in vain.

Patience has more to do with your attitude than with the length of the wait. As you rest in God's character and goodness, He gives you an attitude of expectancy and hope that assures you blessings are coming. If you feel weary, remember that the "proper time" is coming. It may not be today, this week, or even this year, but God is faithful. He sees the seeds of goodness you're planting in your children when no one else does. He is working in your family.

So take a deep breath and ask the Lord to renew your strength. Fix your eyes on His *promise* instead of the *progress* you may or may not see. The harvest *will* come. Keep sowing love, truth, and grace into your children's lives and remember that the Lord of the harvest is with you.

"Only God Himself fully appreciates the influence of a Christian mother in the molding of character in her children."[31]

—Billy Graham

Remember This

Raising children is a process that requires patience, prayer, and trust. As you do the unseen work of motherhood, God is preparing a harvest.

No Comparison

We do not dare to classify or compare ourselves with some who commend themselves. When they measure themselves by themselves and compare themselves with themselves, they are not wise.

2 Corinthians 10:12

Have you felt the soul-sucking sting of comparison? Whether you're watching other moms shine in areas where you struggle or seeing them carry out idyllic routines with seemingly perfect kids, comparing yourself to other moms can make you feel like your efforts are small.

"It's easy to compare yourself to other moms—especially when you're watching their highlight reels on social media," says K-LOVE DJ Amy Baumann. "I had to make an intentional decision to limit my time on social media, so I wouldn't get stuck in the comparison trap."

Paul may not have been a mom, but he talked about comparison. In 2 Corinthians 10:12, he rebuked those who measured their worth against others, saying "they are not wise." *The Message* translation puts it plainly: "In all this comparing and grading and competing, they quite miss the point."

Being a mom isn't about proving your worth; it's about allowing God to work in you, through you, and around you. Fulfilling your role means showing up in your home as the woman God designed you to be. Comparison distracts and diminishes. It mutes the specific calling God has placed on your life.

"What has helped me is talking to God about what is best for my family and asking Him to lead me as a mom," Amy says. She also keeps a journal with a prayer list for each of her sons. "I ask them how I can pray for them and daily take those requests to God. Praying for my kids is something I'm passionate about."

God has equipped you with strengths—tenderness,

creativity, deep listening, compassion, organization—that He uses to shape your children in unique ways. You don't have to be like other moms or measure up to some gold standard. As you faithfully follow Jesus, He will shine through your distinctive strengths to bless your family.

'If you want to claim credit, claim it for God.'
What you say about yourself means nothing in God's work.
It's what God says about you that makes the difference."
—2 Corinthians 10:17–18 (MSG)

Remember This

You don't have to compete, Mom. You only need to be faithful to trust, love, and grow out of your God-given design.

Wholehearted Pursuit

You will seek me and find me
when you seek me with all your heart.

Jeremiah 29:13

The days of a mom are filled with constant demands: meals to make, messes to pick up, and endless needs to meet. As moms, it's easy to feel like there's nothing left for ourselves, let alone a wholehearted pursuit of God. Yet God provides this beautiful promise in Jeremiah. God doesn't hide from us. He wants to be found.

He provides one condition: to seek Him with all our hearts. God knows our propensity for divided hearts. We so easily search for fulfillment in worldly things like social media, the praise of others, TV shows, food, cute home décor, shopping trips, and countless other things. But God asks us to come to Him with our whole hearts, proclaiming that we want what only He can give.

He's not waiting for us to have more time or be more put together. He's waiting for us to seek Him—in the school pickup line, at the kitchen sink, in the quiet moments before bedtime. When we search for Him sincerely, He shows up. This promise isn't just for the super-spiritual—it's for the overwhelmed mom who is simply doing her best.

What does it look like to seek God today? Write down His promises and post them in visible places around your home. When stresses arise, say a short prayer for strength. As you seek the Lord, He promises that He will be found.

"Your purpose and your future depend entirely on the Lord. . . . He will fulfill your purpose and lead you into the future He has for you as you trust Him daily." [32]

—Stormie Omartian

Remember This

God can be found. He doesn't stand at a distance. He wants to be personally involved in your life.

Faith Over Fear

The LORD is good to those
whose hope is in him, to the
one who seeks him.

LAMENTATIONS 3:25

It's been said that having a child is like having a piece of your heart walking around outside your body. That's because motherhood exposes how little control we truly have and the cracks in our coping mechanisms.

Singer Hope Darst understands mothering out of fear. "Fear has always been my Achilles' heel, and it showed up in motherhood," the mom of two daughters admits. "I believed lies about myself like 'I'm not a good mom,' 'I'm making too many mistakes,' or 'I'm going to disappoint my kids.' These false beliefs got in the way of how I made decisions, managed my stress, and, ultimately, how I loved my children."

Hope found herself at a crossroads, knowing fear was robbing her of joy and the ability to steward motherhood in the way she desired. She looked to God's Word for help and worked with a godly counselor to get to the root of the lies.

"It was a long, hard year of really unpacking the burdens I was carrying and laying them at the feet of Jesus," she says. "But He broke the chain of fear of failure in my life, especially in the area of motherhood."

Maybe today God is calling you to release your fear and trust His heart. Maybe you're fearful that you're failing as a mom. Ask God to replace your fear with hope that comes from the Holy Spirit. God sees your fears, your faith, and your prayers. Even when the path feels dark, He is healing, restoring, and walking beside you.

"Motherhood is the job of laying down your own life, allowing Christ to shape and mold you into the best version of yourself, and then taking all of that and pouring it in your children to see them become even greater than you."

—Hope Darst

Remember This

You don't have to be in control. Simply trust the One who is.

36

Proclaiming His Goodness

I will sing the L*ORD's praise,*
for he has been good to me.

Psalm 13:6

Motherhood is a beautiful, chaotic mix of blessings and burdens. Some days, the to-do list feels endless, and your children's needs seem too great to handle. Yet in the middle of the mom madness, God's goodness can be clearly seen.

You've likely glimpsed His goodness: a spiritual conversation with your child on the way to school; a family night where everyone is content in each other's company; the kind stranger who offers you a compliment that encourages you to press on. Even your children are a testimony to His kindness.

The Psalms tell us to sing the Lord's praise. We don't just do this when life is easy or when everything goes right. We praise God because of who He is and what He's done.

In the rigors and dailiness of parenting, it's easy to let our focus drift toward what's not perfect in our lives—the messes, the undone dishes, the missed opportunities. But our children often see something completely different. They find joy in the mundane and discover beauty in the messes. They notice God's hand in ordinary moments and remind us to do the same.

Maybe today you're wrestling with mom guilt or feeling like a failure. Make a mental list of the ways God has shown His goodness to you—just in the past twenty-four hours. His kindness can be found in a warm meal, a hug from your child, a kind word, or a moment of peace. God has been good to you. He is *being* good to you! Let your heart rise in praise today, not because your life is perfect but because He is.

"We want Christ's power to be made perfect
through us weak moms. So we will boast
all the more gladly of our weaknesses,
so that the power of Christ may rest upon us." [33]

—Gloria Furman

Remember This

Think of ways you've seen God's goodness in your life and family and praise Him!

Keep sowing love,
truth, and grace
into your children's
lives and remember
that the Lord
of the harvest
is with you.

Setting the Tone

She opens her mouth with wisdom,
and the teaching of kindness
is on her tongue.

Proverbs 31:26 (ESV)

Maybe you've heard the old saying, "If momma ain't happy, ain't nobody happy." While the phrase may bring a chuckle, it's also extremely true. Moms set the tone of the home.

When Helen Smallbone and her husband, David, moved from Australia to Tennessee with their six children in 1991, money was scarce. The family moved into a small rental house with no electronics, washing machine, or furniture. Helen, pregnant at the time, did her best to turn the family's hardships into fun.

In her book *Behind the Lights,* she writes, "I made beds for the kids by tucking the sheets I had brought with us in and around their winter clothes, and I put a sweater in each pillowcase for their pillows. The kids thought it was a lot of fun—a bit like camping in the house."[34]

In time, a kind and generous church community provided beds, tables, and even a washer and dryer for the family. But Helen's children—among them Luke and Joel Smallbone of For King & Country and singer-songwriter Rebecca St. James—still look back on that lean time with fond memories. They remember how Helen made life feel like an adventure as she depended on God and kept a cheerful demeanor.

As mothers, our presence carries weight. Our words, attitudes, and actions influence our children. When we're stressed or irritable, the entire household feels it. But when we're grounded in the Lord—speaking His life and wisdom—peace fills our home.

Each day, we have a choice. We can allow our emotions to lead in stressful moments, or we can surrender control of the details to God. As we put our trust in Him and spend time in His Word, He will give us the strength to radiate His joy and peace. Off days will come, but a mom anchored in the Lord sends a ripple of faith through the whole house.

> *"The family is the foundation of culture, and the center point of the family is the mother. She holds everything together. A mother, through her children, impacts the world of tomorrow."*[35]
>
> —Helen Smallbone

Remember This

Our words and attitudes deeply impact the atmosphere of the home. When we ground ourselves in Christ, we create an environment of peace and stability where our children can thrive.

The Beauty of Adoption

For he chose us in him before
the creation of the world
to be holy and blameless in his sight.
In love he predestined us for
adoption to sonship through Jesus Christ,
in accordance with his pleasure and will.

Ephesians 1:4–5

Singer-songwriter Nicole C. Mullen comes from a long line of family members who have adopted and fostered children. In her book *It's Never Wrong to Do the Right Thing*, the "On My Knees" singer and writer recalls adopting her son, Max, nearly three decades ago.

"I can't tell you how grateful I am to my son's birth mom for giving him life and for giving me one of my greatest treasures!" Nicole says. "Maxwell is smart, handsome, and godly. I find it funny that [...] of my three children, he resembles me the most!"[36]

Max has been familiar with his adoption story since childhood. As an adult, he sports a tattoo in Hebrew on his upper arm that means "chosen." When asked about it, he answers, "I was chosen twice. Once by God above, and the second time by the family who adopted me."

Nicole views adoption as a picture of how believers are grafted into the family of God. Adoption reflects the redemptive nature of Christ, who offers reconciliation and an eternal inheritance to those who trust in Him. Human adoption is the opportunity for families to give children hope and belonging, honoring God's idea of family and providing a tangible experience of His love.

Whether you are considering placing a child in the arms of another family as a life-affirming option or taking a child into your home through adoption, Nicole emphasizes that courage is required. However, it's courage that will positively change lives, including your own.

"If you are a foster or an adoptive parent, I affirm you. You are courageous to receive a child into your home and hearts. I have watched my family members do the right thing in faith, participating in foster care and becoming adoptive parents. It is truly inspiring to watch!" [37]

—Nicole C. Mullen

Remember This

Adoption reflects Christ's redemption of God's children and provides the opportunity to honor God's idea of family to extend hope and belonging to children in need.

Trusting God When the Plan Changes

In their hearts humans
plan their course, but the LORD
establishes their steps.

PROVERBS 16:9

Many of us are planners. We organize our days, make schedules, and juggle activities, practices, and appointments. We also dream of the future: who our children will become, the trips we might take, and the legacy we'll leave when we're gone. There's nothing wrong with dreaming or planning. In fact, it's often how God stirs our hearts toward what's next.

But sometimes, the plan changes. Maybe you lose a job or must make an unexpected move. Perhaps you receive a scary diagnosis or a pregnancy ends in heartbreak. Maybe your daughter is dealing with mean girls at school, and your momma's heart is breaking. Or the doors you prayed would open stay shut, and you're left staring at a path you didn't choose.

Scripture reminds us that while we plan our course, God establishes our steps. When life feels like it's falling apart, we may wonder if He is still in control. He is. He isn't surprised by the unexpected detour, nor is He scrambling to create a Plan B. He sees the whole picture, and we can be confident that He is working all things together for our good and His glory. While we may never understand the *why,* we can cling to the *Who*—a loving God who comforts us through all of life's challenges.

Whatever you're going through, God is big enough to hold you through it. When plans fail, remember that God is establishing your steps on paths that cultivate deeper faith and lasting joy. When the road is unclear, you can walk hand in hand with the One who knows exactly where you're going.

"The will of God is never exactly what you expect it to be. It may seem to be much worse, but in the end, it's going to be a lot better and a lot bigger."

—Elisabeth Elliot

Remember This

The Creator of the universe has a good plan and a specific path for you to walk. He walks with you and is worthy of your trust.

40

Letting Go

Look carefully then how you walk,
not as unwise but as wise,
making the best use of the time,
because the days are evil.
Ephesians 5:15–16 (ESV)

Have you ever felt pressure to do it all—to get your kids in programs, lessons, practices, and after-school activities?

"You can't do it all," says K-LOVE DJ Amy Baumann. "When I discovered this fact, it was one of the most freeing moments of motherhood." This mom of three teen boys says that when she first had kids, she thought she could do it all—be the best employee, volunteer, wife, and mother.

"I was trying to be everything to everyone," she says, "but my family was suffering." God began showing her the power of stepping back, being content, and letting go of some things. She discovered freedom and peace in free nights home with her family.

"I talked to God and my family and asked what things mattered to them," she says. "We didn't have to do *both* gymnastics and soccer. The boys picked soccer, so we let go of gymnastics." Amy suggests cutting back on activities and even scheduling time for "nothing to do."

"The sweetest moments happen when you stop trying to do it all," she says. "Riding bikes around the neighborhood. Teaching your child how to crack an egg while you're baking cookies. My oldest son tells me his favorite memories are when free afternoons turned into something like stopping at a garage sale where he found a T-ball set. We played for hours in the backyard."

Moms shouldn't feel pressure to do it all. Some of life's richest experiences show up when we slow down and enjoy the moment.

"Let go of the world's expectations and the idea that you have to do it all—have your child in all the things and keep a non-stop schedule. You don't. You have the power of choice. Protect your family."

—Amy Baumann

Remember This

You don't have to do it all. Prioritize what matters most, be willing to let some things go, and enjoy the slower moments God provides.

Looking for Unexpected Gifts

If you, then, though you are evil,
know how to give good gifts
to your children, how much more
will your Father in heaven
give good gifts to those who ask him!

MATTHEW 7:11

Sometimes life doesn't go as planned. Singer-songwriter Tasha Layton knows all about it. In her book *Look What You've Done,* she describes the harrowing experience of giving birth to her son, Levi.

"My labor lasted for over thirty-three hours, and I lost a lot of blood," she writes. "Then, to make matters much worse, Levi came into the world without breath. I can barely describe the helplessness I felt as I watched my newborn son—the child I'd been praying for—fight for his life as the medical team resuscitated him."[38]

Though Levi made a full recovery, Tasha relates that it took almost a year after he was born for her to be able to process the whole experience. At first, she questioned God, feeling like He had betrayed her. One day, while looking through pictures of Levi's early days, she was reminded of all God had done. "Only then could I see clearly that God had protected Levi and me. He'd been with us all along."[39]

When pain and suffering enter our lives, we can be confident that Jesus understands. He is well acquainted with betrayal, loss, sorrow, and grief. And yet, when our dreams get crushed and our hearts get broken, He promises to transform our pain into something new and beautiful. What He gives may look different from what we expected, but all His gifts are good (Matt. 7:11).

God doesn't leave us broken. Through His overcoming power, all can be restored and made even better than before. If something feels damaged in your life today, God sees you. He sent His Son into the brokenness and the mess to make all things new.

"Becoming a parent has taught me more about God than anything I've ever done. I knew God created me and felt unconditional love for me—but now, with this tiny, precious baby in my arms, I understand the concept even more."[40]

—Tasha Layton

Remember This

When we face unplanned detours, we can trust that God wants to give us good gifts that reveal more of His character and let us experience His love.

Heroic Moms

And who knows but that you
have come to your royal position
for such a time as this?
Esther 4:14

Motherhood can feel like a quiet, unseen calling where the days fly by in a blur of laundry, dishes, and being "Uber mom." But just like the Bible heroine Esther, you have been placed where you are on purpose by a powerful God.

In her book *It's Never Wrong to Do the Right Thing*, singer-songwriter Nicole C. Mullen talks about the influence of her godly mother.

"Some of my favorite heroes and sheroes have never worn a cape, but they deserve one," she writes. "One of those people is certainly my mom. Her story may not be found in the history books, and there has not yet been a novel or movie scripted around the deeds she's done. Her name does not appear on the pages of Scripture, but truths reflected in her character do."

Nicole shares in her book how her mother and father married young. By the time her mother, Mary, was twenty-one, she had a three-year-old, an almost two-year-old, and was pregnant with Nicole.

"Nothing about my mother's circumstances was easy or convenient, and I know she had to have been worn out," Nicole says.[41] Yet Mary pressed on, raising three strong, godly women and creating a home filled with grace.

As moms, we may not be royal queens, but we hold the hearts of future world-changers. In a culture that feels increasingly dark and uncertain, your influence as a mother matters more than ever. Every whispered prayer, word of wisdom, and unseen sacrifice is kingdom work. Whether you're helping with homework, driving to yet another soccer game, or soothing your child's hurting heart with words of reassurance, God has placed you in this moment for such a time as this. There's only one you.

"I am forever grateful to my mom for saying yes to the package of grace she needed to parent three young girls. She loved life and taught us to do the same."[42]

—Nicole C. Mullen

Remember This

God equips those He calls, giving you the strength, wisdom, and courage to be the mom your children need.

Each day,
we have a choice.
We can allow our
emotions to lead in
stressful moments,
or we can surrender
control of the
details to God.

Savoring the Seasons

But grow in the grace and knowledge of our Lord and Savior Jesus Christ. To him be glory both now and forever! Amen.

—2 PETER 3:18

It will happen—just like they say. One day you will look up, and the diapers, bottles, and sleepless nights will be replaced with lunchboxes, homework, and "Mom, can I ride up front?" A few years later, you'll be dropping him off at college or walking her down the aisle.

K-LOVE DJ Kelli Caldwell, who has two young adult sons, knows about changing seasons. "One of my favorite parts about being a mom is seeing the men my sons have become," she says. "It's a lovely thing to go from diapers and time-outs to random phone calls 'just because.'"

Ecclesiastes 3:1 says, "There is a time for everything, and a season for every activity under the heavens." If being a mom has taught us anything, it's that those seasons don't ask for permission before they change. They just do.

Kelli has welcomed her current season of motherhood. "I've recently taken solo trips with each of my grown boys," she says. "Jarod and I spent days walking miles in New York City, and Alec and I did an epic road trip to Seattle. We laughed a lot, ate incredible food, and had some deep conversations. If someone had given me a glimpse into those moments when I was in the throes of mothering toddlers, I'm not sure I would have believed it. Hang in there, Momma. One day that kid will be more than your child—he'll be your friend."

You may not enjoy every moment as a mom, but you can savor each season. There's a time to nurse and a time to pack lunches, a time to wait up for teens and a time to outfit a dorm room. Each season, as fleeting as it may be, holds something sacred and worth celebrating.

"My husband and I always prayed that our sons would grow up equipped to leave our home, secure in the knowledge that they are deeply loved by us and by God. I think you can face just about anything when you know this."

—Kelli Caldwell

Remember This

Whatever season you're currently in as a mom, slow down and savor it. Life is meant to change, but through each transition, God is faithful.

You Are Never Alone

Never will I leave you;
never will I forsake you.

Hebrews 13:5

Motherhood can be one of the loneliest full-time jobs in the world. Surrounded by noise (or the silence after bedtime), you may wonder: *Does anyone see me? Does anyone care?*

Scripture brings powerful reassurance: Jesus will never leave you. And His presence isn't dependent on how well-behaved your kids are or how many friends you have. He is with you constantly, even on your loneliest days.

He doesn't want you to stay in isolation though. He designed you for connection! If loneliness is creeping in, that may be the Spirit's gentle nudge to get out and spend time with people. It takes effort to go out instead of staying in for another night of Netflix. But shared laughter and honest conversations are powerful and healing. God designed us to need each other. Community isn't a luxury—it's a lifeline.

If loneliness seems to be clinging to you like a piece of wet toilet paper on your shoe, consider doing something for someone else. Self-pity is a natural trap in hard seasons, but service lifts our eyes off our own struggles and provides the connection of shared experiences. Blessing another mom with a note, a meal, or a word of encouragement can shift your perspective.

When you feel alone, remember that you're not "just a mom." You are a person created with a need for community. Schedule a coffee date with a girlfriend or go out to dinner with your husband. Invest in connecting with others. In lonely moments, remember God sees you. He's beside you, inviting you into the community He created for you.

"The answer to our loneliness is love—
not our finding someone to love us,
but our surrendering to the God who
has always loved us with an everlasting love."[43]

—Elisabeth Elliot

Remember This

The antidote for loneliness is connection with God and others. In the busy season of being a mom, look for ways to form authentic friendships and community.

45

Joy Will Come

Weeping may stay for the night,
but rejoicing comes in the morning.
—Psalm 30:5

Losing a child is an unimaginable sorrow. Lynn Wilson, mother of "My Jesus" singer Anne Wilson, experienced this when her son, Jacob, died in a car accident at twenty-three.

"Losing my son was one of the most devastating experiences I have ever walked through," she says. "In this immense grief, I had to invite the Lord to meet me in my deepest pain."

Jacob's passing inadvertently launched his sister's music career when she sang at his funeral and was later discovered through a video posted online. The family experienced the unique combination of heartache and loss side by side with new dreams and hope. Anne's music ministry continues to be a source of joy for Lynn, her husband, and their other daughter, Elizabeth.

Lynn encourages grieving moms to pour out every feeling to God—including anger and sorrow—without holding anything back. "God isn't offended by your questions or your honest prayers," she says. "Psalm 34:18 tells us, 'The Lord is close to the brokenhearted and saves those who are crushed in spirit.' He meets you where you are and comforts you in your suffering."

In the darkest moments of sorrow, when grief feels too heavy to bear, God's tender care surrounds us. Though we may weep through long, sleepless nights, a morning of joy is coming. God doesn't rush our grief—He sits with us in it. In grief and loss, God's love is often expressed through the quiet presence of others—an embrace, a prayer, or shared tears. These tangible comforts offer us glimpses of His heart.

Though the night may feel endless, you can be certain morning is coming—and with it, the joy of knowing you are held by a God who deeply cares for every part of your story.

"Prayer opens the door for His presence to wrap around your broken heart like a gentle embrace. He will renew your strength. God is holding your child in His eternal love, and you can cling to the hope that one day He will wipe every tear from your eyes."

—Lynn Wilson

Remember This

For mothers who have lost a child, the pain is deep and unspeakable. Yet in the dark valleys, God often reveals His nearness most profoundly.

46

You Need a Tribe

Therefore encourage one another
and build each other up,
just as in fact you are doing.

1 Thessalonians 5:11

"You can't do it alone!" is a sentiment K-LOVE DJ Amy Baumann firmly believes. "Yes, you have Jesus," she says, "but you have to find friends and family who *live* life with you and see your mess, or you'll go completely crazy."

As moms, we need women in our lives—sisters, mentors, and friends—who will be there when life gets tough. We're not meant to handle the stresses of motherhood alone.

"You need people you can vent with, pray with, and who will encourage you," Amy says. "Those moms are your lifeline when you feel like you're losing it."

On days when your tank feels empty and your spirit feels frayed, seek out those in your tribe. Laugh over a cup of coffee while the kids play, grab dinner with a fellow mom of teenagers to compare notes, or join a Bible study with other women you can trust. True friends come in all ages. They show up in many places—at your child's school, in your moms' group, or even on your street.

Motherhood is beautiful and exhausting. You need fellow warrior moms to witness your life and help you live out your sacred calling. If you're having a hard day, remember that you're not alone. Jesus is with you; He is your strength and your rock. But He's also placed people around you to build you up and do life together.

"Succeeding at motherhood is a lot about perspective
and community. Even though it's hard,
it's also one of the greatest gifts and
privileges of our lives to be a MOM!"

—Amy Baumann

Remember This

Motherhood is messy, and you need encouragement, support, and prayer. Don't try to do it alone.

Releasing Fear, Embracing Faith

For God gave us a spirit not of fear
but of power and love and self-control.
—2 Timothy 1:7 (ESV)

If you've ever felt paralyzed by fear as a mom, you're not alone. From the moment our babies are placed in our arms, the world floods us with warnings and recommendations, milestones to track, and dangers to avoid. Each decision can feel like it carries lifelong consequences. It's enough to make even the steadiest heart tremble. And when something does go wrong—a frightening diagnosis, a serious accident, or an unexpected trip to the ER—those fears move from hypothetical to heart-wrenching reality.

We may live in a scary world, but Scripture tells us that fear is not from God. Instead, He gives us a spirit that is powerful, rooted in love, and anchored in self-control. We don't have to live constantly bracing for the next crisis. When life feels uncertain, we can parent from a place of peace and empowerment.

Even when our children are healthy and thriving, life can be scary. And at some point, we must release them into the world to make their own decisions and take on their own challenges. But first, we must release them to God. We won't always be right there to watch their every move, but God will be—just as He is right now.

In motherhood, there are many things outside our control. But we serve a God who sees everything and holds our children in His hands. We can breathe deeply and release our kids into His care, knowing He loves them even more than we do. We aren't promised a worry-free journey through motherhood, but we are promised God's presence, power, and love.

"A perfect faith would lift us absolutely above fear."[44]

—Elisabeth Elliot

Remember This—

Reining in fear requires love, reliance on God's power, and self-control. When you realize that God loves your children even more than you do, you can release them into His care and trust Him without fear.

The Power of Traditions

These commandments that I give you today are to be on your hearts. Impress them on your children. Talk about them when you sit at home and when you walk along the road, when you lie down and when you get up.

DEUTERONOMY 6:6–7

Family traditions come in many forms—from cultural practices to faith-community rituals to individual family celebrations. Research shows that traditions strengthen family bonds, increase children's happiness, create lasting memories, and instill family values. No wonder God used feasts and celebrations to help Israelite parents pass on their faith to their children!

Singer-songwriter Naomi Raine shares how the tradition of making dinner helps her feel close to her kids. "My favorite thing about being a mom is cooking the kids their favorite meals," she says. "I love the joy I get seeing their joy in watching me cook and eating their favorite meal."

Spending time together in the kitchen is a simple family tradition that makes a big impact. Family rituals don't have to be complicated. They can be ordinary, everyday practices like reading books at bedtime, attending church together, having pizza on Friday nights, or employing inside jokes or affectionate nicknames. Even holiday traditions can teach our children about God and help them experience His goodness.

Psalm 34:8 says, "Taste and see that the Lord is good; blessed is the one who takes refuge in him." Traditions help our children experience the sweetness and beauty that comes from a life centered on Jesus.

What are your favorite family traditions? What daily and weekly habits make your family unique? How can you use these rituals to reinforce matters of faith? As moms, we have the special role of creating meaningful moments our children will always remember—moments that leave a powerful family legacy.

> *"God's purpose and calling for mothers is to love,*
> *nurture, and care for their children and*
> *raise them up to serve, fear and worship the Lord*
> *as good stewards of everything He's provided."*
> —Naomi Raine

Remember This

Family traditions don't have to be complicated. Family rituals bring us together and show our kids that life centered on Jesus is sweet.

Jesus
will never
leave you.

49 Motherhood Is a Battlefield

Finally, be strong in the Lord and in his mighty power. Put on the full armor of God, so that you can take your stand against the devil's schemes. For our struggle is not against flesh and blood, but against the rulers, against the authorities, against the powers of this dark world and against the spiritual forces of evil in the heavenly realms.

Ephesians 6:10–12

Have you ever had a day when it felt like the whole world was out to get you? A mom friend has a funny T-shirt that reads, "Why y'all trying to test the Jesus in me?"

Relatable, right? From toddler tantrums to teenage attitudes, it's clear we have an enemy who's watching for moments when our guard is down. He looks for times when you're exhausted, distracted, or discouraged to pull off his destructive schemes.

In Ephesians, Paul reminds us that our struggle isn't against the people around us—not even those under our own roof. The real battle is spiritual. And God offers us powerful protection! He's given us His armor not just to survive motherhood, but to live it out with strength, purpose, and victory.

Every morning, before the chaos begins, you can suit up with:

- The belt of truth
- The breastplate of righteousness
- The shield of faith
- The footwear of readiness with the gospel of peace
- The helmet of salvation
- The sword of the Spirit
- Prayer

God has given you powerful weapons to stand firm in the spiritual battle. The enemy wants your family. He wants to steal your peace. But you are a strong warrior, armed with truth, righteousness, faith, peace, salvation, the Holy Spirit, and prayer. So suit up every single day and fight for your children, your marriage, and your faith. The Lord has equipped you, and you fight in His strength and power.

Be on your guard; stand firm in the faith;
be courageous; be strong.
—1 Corinthians 16:13

Remember This

God has given us His armor—not just to survive motherhood but to thrive in it. Put on His armor every day and fight in His strength.

Hope for Hard Days

He tends his flock like a shepherd:
He gathers the lambs in his arms
and carries them close to his heart;
he gently leads those that have young.

Isaiah 40:11

Have you ever had a bad mom day? You lost your temper and yelled at your "little blessings." You stumbled into the kitchen Monday morning only to discover you were out of coffee. The car wouldn't start, the house was a mess, the dog threw up, and not a shoe could be found when it was time to leave the house. We've all been there.

Regardless of your season of motherhood, stress is inevitable. It comes with the job. Singer-songwriter and boy mom of two, Rachael Lampa, has advice for hard days: "Feel it! Feel the weariness and let it run its course through your head, your heart, and your body. Don't be ashamed of the hard stuff. It's part of the process; it forces us to draw close to God and find comfort."

God understands the stress that comes with being a mom. Motherhood is a season of not only attending to your own needs but also managing the needs—and demands—of many others. Isaiah 40:11 offers us this precious promise: "He gathers the lambs in his arms and carries them close to his heart; He gently leads those that have young."

It's comforting to know that God cares about our "lambs" and holds them close to His heart. Not only that, He notices our special role as mothers caring for them. He knows us intimately and understands the path we're walking. He sees every sacrifice and act of service. He sees each tear.

In the stretching moments of motherhood, you can rest in that knowledge. Your gentle Shepherd leads you with compassion; be gentle with yourself today, knowing He is with you.

"As moms we are called to mirror the patience, grit, passion, compassion, and love of God. We get to show our children that it's okay for this life to be hard sometimes. And we get to be the safe place they return to again and again as they figure it all out."

—Rachael Lampa

Remember This

On stressful mom days, trust the leading of your Good Shepherd and draw near to Him for comfort. Point your children to Jesus, who is there for them when life is hard.

The God of Possible

Jesus looked at them and said,
"With man this is impossible,
but with God all
things are possible."
MATTHEW 19:26

Motherhood is a beautiful calling, but as our children grow into teens and young adults, it can also feel like a battlefield of faith. As we watch them wrestle with their identities, decisions about the future, relationship choices, and even with God Himself, it's easy to feel helpless. We may wonder whether the seeds we've sown will take root.

Jesus reminded us that what is impossible for us is entirely possible with God. That's why we continue praying for our children and never give up. We can't force them to follow Christ, avoid sin, or make wise decisions. We can't protect them from every consequence or fix everything that breaks. But we serve a God who can.

As mothers, we're called to raise our children in the knowledge of God and help them walk in His ways. We offer wisdom, provide love, set boundaries, and model faith. But after we've done all that is possible, we must place the rest in God's hands. He is the One who specializes in changing and healing hearts.

As we put the work into raising our kids, we can trust that God hears our prayers and sees our efforts. He's always working behind the scenes. Maybe your teen is struggling with identity or relationships. Perhaps your adult child is drifting or dealing with addiction. Don't give up! God is not finished writing their stories. What feels like an impossible situation today is an opportunity for God to show His power tomorrow. Nothing is impossible with Him!

"We mothers must take care of the possible and trust God for the impossible."[45]

—Ruth Bell Graham

Remember This

Be faithful with what has been entrusted to you and surrender what is out of your control. God has a plan and a purpose for your child, and with Him, all things are possible.

Winning the Mental Game

And we take captive every thought
to make it obedient to Christ.

2 Corinthians 10:5

As moms, our minds rarely rest. From meal planning and laundry to school projects, doctor's appointments, and a thousand little worries in between, our thoughts are constantly spinning. Add in the emotional weight of parenting, and it's easy to find ourselves tangled in a web of self-condemnation, fear, comparison, or even resentment.

Maybe you've caught yourself thinking, *I'm failing as a mom.* Or, *Why is her life easier than mine?* Maybe you replay a harsh word you spoke to your child or obsess over a parenting mistake. These thoughts might seem small, but over time they build false beliefs that distance us from the truth of who God is and who we are in Him.

God's Word tells us to take every thought captive and make it obedient to Christ. This doesn't mean ignoring hard feelings or pretending everything's fine when it's not. Instead, we recognize when our thoughts are not aligned with God's truth and choose to replace them with His promises.

> When your thoughts whisper, *You're not enough,* God says, "My grace is sufficient for you" (2 Cor. 12:9).
>
> When worry overtakes your heart, God says, "Cast all your anxiety on him" (1 Pet. 5:7).
>
> When comparison creeps in, God says you are "fearfully and wonderfully made" (Ps. 139:14).

Taking thoughts captive is a daily—sometimes hourly—discipline. But it's also a path to freedom. As your mind is renewed, your heart is strengthened. You'll find more peace in your day, more patience with your kids, and more joy in the little moments of motherhood.

"Most of all, let the Word of God fill you
and renew your mind every day.
When our minds are on Christ,
Satan has little room to maneuver."[46]

—Billy Graham

Remember This

Invite God to root out negative thoughts and replace them with the life-giving mindset of Christ.

Trust God in Disappointments

Not only so, but we also glory in our sufferings,
because we know that suffering produces
perseverance; perseverance, character;
and character, hope. And hope does
not put us to shame, because God's love
has been poured out into our hearts through
the Holy Spirit, who has been given to us.

Romans 5:3–5

Disappointment enters our children's lives in many forms: not making the team, being overlooked for a special honor, not being invited to the party, or being betrayed by a friend.

When disappointment strikes, our first impulse may be to try to "fix it." As we did when they were little and got a boo-boo, we may rush into rescue mode, attempting to soothe their hurting hearts and smooth out the speed-bumps of life.

Whether our children's disappointment stems from the consequence of an unwise choice, an unforeseen obstacle, or a heartbreaking setback, as moms, we long to ease their suffering and take away the pain. It's true that we hold great power to comfort and reassure our children. However, we can also trust that God will use disappointment in their lives to shape their character and help them grow.

As we help our children understand that disappointment is a part of life, we teach them that while unmet expectations are painful, they can trust that God has a purpose in them.

As moms, many of us have experienced the loss of dreams and witnessed how God has redeemed our pain and disappointment. Perhaps we have watched Him give us a new ministry out of a broken dream or unmet expectation. We need to tell our children these stories of God's grace. When our children watch us turn our disappointments into opportunities to trust God, they will do the same.

Don't be afraid to normalize disappointment. But also don't forget to proclaim God's power to redeem suffering and make our lives more beautiful than we could imagine.

"I used to worry that my children would resent the radical lifestyle we lived. I prayed and the Lord imprinted on my mind a promise: 'I will teach them what they need to know.' Today, each of my children are following Jesus and have the skills they need for their different callings. It has touched me deeply to stand on a promise given by God and see Him fulfill it!"

—Helen Smallbone

Remember This

You can trust that God will use adversity in your child's life to shape his character and help him grow. Stand firm on His promises!

I Just Want to Be with You

Here I am! I stand at the door and knock.
If anyone hears my voice and opens the door,
I will come in and eat with that person,
and they with me.

Revelation 3:20

Have you ever noticed how young children crave our presence? There's something beautiful (and sometimes exhausting) about the way they seek us out. Whether we're cooking dinner, answering emails, or even trying to grab a quiet moment in the bathroom, they find us. They climb into our laps, chitchat about their lives, or simply insist on being near us. Presence is their love language.

The persistent, loving pursuit of our children is a reminder of how we should desire our heavenly Father. Do we want to be with Him the way our children want to be with us? Do we long to sit in His presence each day? Is He our number-one desire?

How amazing that Jesus knocks on the door of your heart! He's knocking, eager to sit with you, share life, hear about your day, and speak to your heart. The Creator of the universe is waiting for you to open the door—not for a lecture, but for fellowship.

Too often, we miss the intimacy with the Father that's available to us. We allow ourselves to desire other things, such as comfort and status, that will never truly satisfy. All the while, our Father is waiting for us to come to Him and just be with Him.

Sitting with God daily requires discipline and desire. You must set aside the to-do list and the worries of the day long enough to read God's Word and respond. But the more time you spend in His presence, the more your desire to be with Him will grow.

Our days are full—sometimes to overflowing. Our days are full - sometimes overflowing, "I just want to be with You."

"Your hope as a parent is not found in your power, your wisdom, your character, your experience, or your success, but in this one thing alone: the presence of your Lord."

—Paul David Tripp

Remember This

Jesus is knocking. He wants to have fellowship with you, hear your struggles, and share your burdens.

Nothing
is impossible
with Him!

The Power of a Praying Momma

The prayer of a righteous person
is powerful and effective.

James 5:16

In her song "Praying Woman," artist Anne Wilson paints a picture of the quiet strength of a mother who stands in the gap for her family through prayer. Based in part on Anne's mom, Lynn, the song points to the truth that some of the most powerful battles a mom will ever fight happen on her knees.

"When you pray, you're not just speaking words; you are waging war on behalf of your children," Lynn declares. "You're inviting the Holy Spirit's power into their lives by speaking protection over them and declaring God's promises over them."

Motherhood often comes with an abundance of burdens and concerns for our children—their futures, their health, their relationships. "God knows their needs, their fears, and the battles that are on the horizon," Lynn says. "Prayer places all of this into the hands of the Almighty, the One who loves them even more than you do."

Your persistence in prayer is a gift to your children. Every time you choose to pray instead of panic, you are bringing God deeper into the folds of your family. As an experienced "praying woman," Lynn offers this advice: "Mommas, you are warriors for your child, and your earnest prayers reach further than your arms ever could. They cover your children whether they are right beside you or miles away."

If today feels overwhelming, remember the power you possess. You are a praying woman! Chains break when mommas intercede for their children, and generations are changed by such faith.

"Don't underestimate the power of your prayers, Momma. When the battle feels heavy, your prayers are a shield, a covering, and a weapon. They need not be eloquent or wordy. Speak exactly what's on your mind and heart. Prayer closes the gap between your weakness and God's strength."

—Lynn Wilson

Remember This

God isn't looking for perfect mothers—He's looking for praying ones.

Beautiful Momma

You are altogether beautiful,
my darling; there is
no flaw in you.
Song of Songs 4:7

Have you noticed how motherhood has a way of reshaping us? Our bodies may change but so do our hearts, priorities, and even how we view ourselves. You may glance at old photos and see a younger version of yourself—toned, rested, put together—and feel a pang of loss. These days, your reflection may reveal tired eyes, messy hair, and a body that carries the evidence of sleepless nights and endless giving. It's easy to wonder if your beauty is a thing of the past.

Rest assured, beauty is not behind you. In fact, it's

shining more brightly today than ever. You were made in the image of a beautiful God who delights in you—not only when you look put together, but when you're pouring yourself out in love.

Proverbs reminds us that physical "beauty is fleeting," yet God uses beauty to describe His people. Song of Songs 4:7 speaks these tender words: "You are altogether beautiful, my darling; there is no flaw in you." This is about how God sees you—lovely, radiant, beautiful. This kind of beauty doesn't fade with time or the changings of seasons. It shines when you sit on the floor playing blocks with your toddler, when you hold your hurting "big kid" close, and when you sacrifice sleep, time, and energy to support your struggling teen.

Though you may not always recognize your beauty, your children do. When they look at you, they see affection, safety, and love. They aren't comparing you to a filtered image; they are experiencing beauty in its purest form—presence, care, and unconditional love.

Next time you think, *I'm just going to look like a mom now,* remember this: Moms are beautiful! You are beloved by God, not because you've kept up appearances, but because you are His precious daughter.

"No language can express the power and beauty and heroism of a mother's love."

—Edwin Chapin

Remember This—

You are created for beauty. God made you in His image to reflect His beauty to those around you.

Leading Hearts to Living Water

My people have committed two sins:
They have forsaken me,
the spring of living water,
and have dug their own cisterns,
broken cisterns that cannot hold water.

Jeremiah 2:13

As moms, we want so desperately to get it right. We long to be steady, godly examples—calm in the chaos. But our parenting doesn't always reflect that ideal. When stress mounts and our emotions get the best of us, we may find ourselves modeling the *opposite* of what we want our children to become.

Like it or not, our children are always watching us. They notice how we respond to pain, conflict, and failure. When we're stressed or anxious, do we turn to the Lord in prayer, or do we seek comfort in food, entertainment, or a little retail therapy? When people hurt us, do we bad-mouth them, or do we choose grace and self-control? When we speak harshly to our kids, do we hold our ground in pride, or do we say we're sorry and ask for forgiveness?

In the book of Jeremiah, God rebukes His people for two key failures: forsaking Him—the spring of living water—and turning to their own empty solutions. At times, we lead our children toward "broken cisterns," teaching them that temporary fixes and worldly comforts can soothe their pain when only God can.

Thankfully, our failures don't have the final word. Missteps are opportunities to show our children how to turn back to God. As moms, we can confess, ask forgiveness, and point our children not to *our* perfection but to the perfect Savior.

Your influence is powerful, Mom, but its overall effect doesn't hinge on a flawless performance. Success is found in humility, honesty, and a commitment to do what's right. You may not know how to fix every problem, but you *can* lead your children to the One who is the solution—Jesus, the spring of living water.

"Motherhood isn't about being perfect and never messing up; it's about knowing there is grace and mercy for all our mistakes. Ultimately, my kids don't need a perfect mother. They have a perfect Savior in Jesus. They need an imperfect mother who is completely dependent on God, humble enough to admit when she's wrong, and one who consistently points them to Christ."

—Hope Darst

Remember This

Our lives should point our children to the true hope and help found in Jesus. Our failures are opportunities to model for our children how to turn back to God.

Connecting with Grandparents

Children's children are a crown
to the aged, and parents
are the pride of their children.

Proverbs 17:6

Motherhood is a journey of planting seeds of love, faith, patience, and wisdom in our children. One of the most beautiful and often overlooked gardens in which these seeds can flourish is between children and their grandparents. Proverbs reminds us that grandchildren are a "crown to the aged."

It's interesting how both children and the older generation move at a slower pace. They make natural companions on the road of life. Whether your parents—or other grandparent types—live across the street or across the country, intentionally inviting them into your children's lives can be a life-giving gift for everyone.

These vital relationships don't happen by chance. They are built step by step through shared meals, video chats, and by slowing your pace so everyone can walk together. Encourage your kids to get to know their grandparents by asking them questions and discussing their hobbies and talents. Let them see the people behind the titles "Grandma" and "Grandpa." Allow Grandpa to show your son how to shine shoes or Grandma to teach him how to make a favorite family recipe. These small, shared moments often become lasting memories.

Holidays also offer opportunities to draw close. Invite your kids to participate in longtime family traditions or sample special foods their grandparents enjoy. Catering to the older generation teaches children flexibility, honor, and the value of togetherness.

As Paul wrote to Timothy, deep faith is passed from one generation to the next. As a mom, you can encourage that process as you connect your kids with the older generation. Then when your children come home glowing from time spent with their grandparents, be grateful for memories and lessons that will last a lifetime.

"I am reminded of your sincere faith, which first lived in your grandmother Lois and in your mother Eunice and, I am persuaded, now lives in you also."

—2 Timothy 1:5 (NIV)

Remember This

Be intentional to nurture the bond between your children and their grandparents. Blending generations brings joy to everyone involved.

Our Unshakable Hope

Therefore, with minds that are alert
and fully sober, set your hope on
the grace to be brought to you when
Jesus Christ is revealed at his coming.

—1 Peter 1:13

As moms, we are no strangers to pressure. Each day brings a new set of tasks, expectations, and emotional demands—school pickup lines, meal planning, cooking, cleaning, and the list goes on. We are constantly striving after something.

Peter tells us to prepare our minds for action, be self-controlled, and set our hope on Christ. Those words resonate for moms. Our lives *demand* action and self-control. But more importantly, our hope must be fully set on the grace found in Jesus Christ—*fully*, not partially. That means we must place every ounce of our hope in Him.

Anything else we hope in can, and will, fall apart. Relationships disappoint, kids struggle, ministries falter, and dreams get delayed. When we place our hope in circumstances, disillusionment lurks around the corner. We're shaken when our teen becomes rebellious or our child develops a medical condition. We're anxious when our marriage hits a crisis or a friend betrays us. When Christ is the object of our hope, storms will come, but He will be our solid rock who does not disappoint.

When life isn't going according to plan, rest in the truth that Jesus is your glorious hope. No matter what obstacles or setbacks you encounter in this life, you have eternal joy set before you in the next. He is pursuing your children, working in your relationships, hearing your prayers, and transforming you into His image.

"My hope does not rest in the affairs of this world. It rests in Christ who is coming again." [47]

—Billy Graham

Remember This

Don't just invite Jesus into your plans—*make* Him the plan. Trust the One who never, ever fails.

He'll Finish What He Started

Being confident of this, that he who began a good work in you will carry it on to completion until the day of Christ Jesus.

Philippians 1:6

Have you ever looked around at the mess of motherhood and wondered if you're really accomplishing anything? Between half-folded piles of laundry, a sink full of dishes, and the pressure to "do it all," it's easy to feel like you're falling short and failing to meet a quota. Maybe you started the day with good intentions—in prayer and with purpose—but somewhere around mid-morning things unraveled.

We all leave things unfinished, but God doesn't. In Philippians, Paul reminds us that the One who began a good work in you will carry it on to completion. Here's the thing: God isn't surprised by your bad days, your tears, or even your doubts. In fact, He works all things together to accomplish His will and create beauty in your life.

You're not the one responsible for completing the work—He is. The same God who called you to be a mom is the One who empowers you daily, even when you feel weak or inadequate. Every quiet moment of surrender, every whispered prayer for patience, and every selfless act of love is part of His good work in you.

So be encouraged, Momma. You don't have to be perfect to fulfill your calling and be used by God. He sees your effort and your desire to raise your children well, and He's not done with you yet. Whether you're up feeding a newborn at 2 a.m., taxiing your kids to practices and rehearsals, or getting your teen ready for his first date, God is working. He will finish what He started in you and in your children.

"We are, first and foremost, beloved sons and daughters of the most high God. And so, being a mom has helped me remember that before I'm even a mom, I'm God's daughter, and He's going to take such good care of me, and He's going to take such good care of my kids, too."[48]

—Ellie Holcomb

Remember This

God never leaves work unfinished. You can trust that He will bring to fruition everything He has planted in you. Trust the process and lean on His strength.

Notes

1. Dr. James Dobson, "Mothers and Sons," *Dr. James Dobson Family Institute* (blog), June 9, 2015, https://www.drjamesdobson.org/blogs/mothers-and-sons-2/.

2. CeCe Winans, *Believe for It: Passing on Faith to the Next Generation* (K-LOVE Books, 2022), 97.

3. Winans, *Believe for It*, 105.

4. Kristen Ivy and Reggie Joiner, *Parenting Your Kindergartner: A Guide to Making the Most of the "Look at Me!" Phase* (Orange Books, 2017).

5. Paul David Tripp, *Parenting: 14 Gospel Principles That Can Radically Change Your Family* (Crossway, 2024), 188.

6. Linda Wooten, *A Mother's Thoughts* (2014).

7. Charles Haddon Spurgeon, "The Sunday-School and the Scriptures," *Metropolitan Tabernacle Pulpit*, vol. 31, sermon preached October 18, 1885, accessed via The Spurgeon Library, https://www.spurgeon.org/resource-library/sermons/the-sunday-school-and-the-scriptures/.

8. Tasha Layton, *Look What You've Done: The Lies We Believe & The Truth That Sets Us Free* (K-LOVE Books, 2023) 207.

9. Layton, *Look What You've Done*, 208.

10. Helen Smallbone, *Behind the Lights: The Extraordinary Adventure of a Mum and Her Family* (K-LOVE Books, 2022) 202.

11. Rachael Elmore, "The Motherhood Vow," *Proverbs 31 Ministries*, May 9, 2023, https://proverbs31.org/read/devotions/full-post/2023/05/09/the-motherhood-vow.

12. Taylor, Madison, and Logan Cain, *We're So Blessed: Forty Days of Devotions and Activities for the Whole Family* (K-LOVE Books, 2025).

13. Cain, *We're So Blessed*, 84–85.

14. Michale Foust, "Rachael Lampa Honors Son with Down Syndrome in Uplifting New Song 'Superpowers,'" *Crosswalk.com*, March 24, 2025, https://www.crosswalk.com/headlines/contributors/michael-foust/rachael-lampa-honors-son-with-down-syndrome-in-uplifting-new-song-superpowers.html.

15. Rachel Lampa (@rachaellampa), "Happy birthday Leo!!! You are a dream boy and all things good and all things love and all things YOU!," Instagram, October 28, 2024, https://www.instagram.com/reel/DBrAg-Zap5k3/?igsh=MXE0dnZvbTY5bXZjNQ==.

16. Rachel Denison, "God's Care for Postpartum Mom," *RisenMotherhood*, September 10, 2020, https://www.risenmotherhood.com/articles/gods-care-for-postpartum-moms.

17. Winans, *Believe for It*, 166–167.

18. Winans, *Believe for It*, 166.

19. Michael Kwan, "Sunday Snippet: Washington Irving (1783–1859)," *beyond the rhetoric* (blog), May 8, 2011, https://btr.michaelkwan.com/2011/05/08/sunday-snippet-washington-irving-1783-1859/.

20. Billy Graham, "The influence of a mother upon the lives of her children," Facebook post, May 12, 2024, https://www.facebook.com/photo/?fbid=1001687521325181&set=a.259218252238782.

21. Winans, *Believe for It*, 147–148.

22. Winans, *Believe for It*, 143.

23. Kelsey Borresen, "The Part of a Mom's Mental Load That We Don't Talk About Enough," *Huffpost*, updated March 26, 2024, https://www.huffpost.com/entry/mom-mental-load_l_63f7a67ee4b0616708e04d9a.

24. Lysa TerKeurst (@LysaTerKeurst), "Motherhood is a million little moments," Twitter (now X), May 7, 2016, https://x.com/LysaTerKeurst/status/728950279585054720.

25. Nicole C. Mullen, *It's Never Wrong to Do the Right Thing*, (Esther Press, 2025) 123–124.

26. Mullen, *It's Never Wrong*.

27. Mullen, *It's Never Wrong*.

28. Mullen, *It's Never Wrong*.

29. Mullen, *It's Never Wrong*, 124.

30. Sally Clarkson (@sally.clarkson), "I always wanted to be a hero," Instagram post, November 20, 2023, https://www.instagram.com/p/Cz3fgDRuyLx/.

NOTES

31. Billy Graham, "The Influence of a Mother," *Billy Graham Evangelistic Association* (devotional), May 8, taken from Joan Winmill Brown, ed. and comp., Day by Day with Billy Graham (Worldwide Publications, 1976), 70, https://billygraham.org/devotions/a-mothers-influence.
32. Stormie Omartian (@stormieormartian), "Your purpose and your future depend entirely on . . .", Instagram, January 24, 2025, https://www.instagram.com/p/DFNm6olzfM3/?utm_source=ig_web_copy_link&igsh=MzRlODBiNWFlZA==.
33. "Weekend A La Carte (May 13)," A La Carte (blog), *Challies*, May 13, 2023, https://www.challies.com/a-la-carte/weekend-a-la-carte-may-13/.
34. Smallbone, *Behind the Lights*, 53–54.
35. Smallbone, *Behind the Lights*, 196.
36. Mullen, *It's Never Wrong*, 50–51.
37. Mullen, *It's Never Wrong*, 51.
38. Layton, *Look What You've Done*, 181–182.
39. Layton, *Look What You've Done*, 183.
40. Layton, *Look What You've Done*, 184.
41. Mullen, *It's Never Wrong*, 217.
42. Mullen, *It's Never Wrong*, 219.
43. Elisabeth Elliot, *The Path of Loneliness* (Grand Rapids, MI: Revell, 2007).
44. "Elisabeth Elliot on George MacDonald," *The Works of George MacDonald* (blog), February 19, 2022, https://www.worksofmacdonald.com/georges-admirers/2022/2/19/elisabeth-elliot-on-george-macdonald#:~:text=%E2%80%9CIn%20George%20MacDonald's%20Sir%20Gibbie,the%20ice%20of%20unkindness%20forms.%E2%80%9D.
45. Ruth Bell Graham, *Prodigals and Those Who Love Them: Words of Encouragement for Those Who Wait* (Grand Rapids, MI: Baker Books, 2008) 118.
46. Billy Graham, *Wisdom for Each Day: Daily Devotions to Guide Your Life and Grow Your Faith* (Nashville, TN: Thomas Nelson, 2008).
47. Billy Graham, *The Jesus Generation* (Grand Rapids, MI: Zondervan, 1971) 177.
48. Lauren McKeithen, "Ellie Holcomb Says Motherhood Gave Her a New Perspective on God's Grace," *beliefnet.com*, June 2024, https://www.beliefnet.com/columnists/strongermarriages/2024/06/ellie-holcomb-says-motherhood-gave-her-a-new-perspective-on-gods-grace.html.

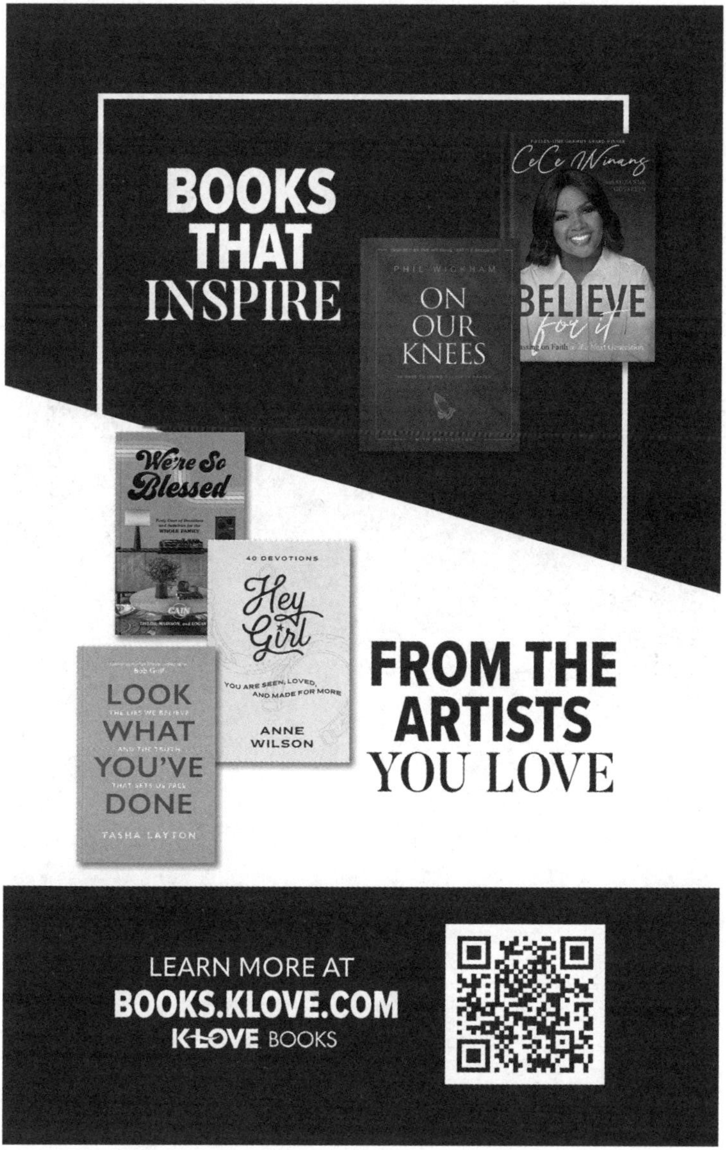